My 12 Rules for Living

1. Make your own happiness… *you're the only one responsible for it;*

2. If a door shuts… *learn to pick locks so you can open another;*

3. If someone is rude… *kill them with kindness;*

4. Take care of your health… *so you don't create an unexpected loss;*

5. Plan for the future or the end… *relieve loved ones of wondering what you want;*

6. Do the best you can with what you have… *even if it's not much;*

7. If someone hurts you… *find a way to get even* – in a classy lady-like way, of course;

8. Life is short… *tell your family and friends you love them as often as possible because there may not be a tomorrow;*

9. Respect your elders… *they hold wisdom;*

10. Protect and direct the youngsters… *growing up is hard work;*

11. Ask for what you want… *those who don't ask don't get;*

12. Accept others for what and who they are in spite of differences… *I don't have to love everything about what you do to love you.*

All rules are subject to change without notice…

The Immortal Alcoholic's Wife

Linda Bartee Doyne

aka Linda Jane Riley

DEDICATION

This book is dedicated to all persons who are now or have been in the situation of living inside the insane chaos of caring for an alcoholic. While each circumstance is different, we are just the same.

TABLE OF CONTENTS

PART THREE

ACKNOWLEDGMENTS

I have many people to thank for helping me make this book possible. Gil, Ann, Georgie, Carrot, Karen and many others, have all served as advisors and editors to help me streamline my thoughts and make it all make sense.

THANK YOU TO ALL OF YOU!!

I also owe a huge debt of gratitude to my blog readers who inspired me to write about my journey from a young girl taking care of her grandmother to the senior citizen caretaking her alcoholic husband. If it had not been for you, I might not have thought anyone would be interested in my life.

THANK YOU!!

The journey has been long and complicated. I have a giant-sized family and extended family. You will find a Cast of Characters to help you follow along as far as who is who and who is related to who and how. There is also a Geographical Road Map to help you follow where I have lived. My brother lovingly refers to me as the family gypsy – and I suppose he is absolutely right.

I hope this book inspires you to cry, laugh, and most of all know that if you're the caretaker of an end-stage alcoholic –

YOU ARE NOT ALONE IN THE ABSENCE OF SANITY

CAST OF CHARACTERS

THE LOGANS

Grandma – My father's mother

Samuel Logan -- My father

Caroline Logan -- My mother

Richard Logan – the oldest child of Samuel and Caroline Logan

Carrot Logan – Richard's wife and Linda's best friend

LINDA JANE LOGAN RILEY – second child of Samuel and Caroline Logan

Riley Riley – Father of Linda's first child, married Linda Jane in 1980

Brian Riley (1967)– son of Riley and Linda Jane

Tina Saunders – fiancé of Brian Riley

Peter Newly – Linda's first husband, father of Linda's daughter, div.1972

Alea Newly Jones (1971) – daughter of Linda

John Jones – husband of Alea

Ryan Jones – son of Alea Newly Jones

Nicole Jones – wife of Ryan Jones

Emily Jones – daughter of Ryan & Nicole

Mikey Jones – son of Ryan & Nicole

Charlie Logan – third child of Samuel and Caroline Logan

Evan Logan – fourth child of Samuel and Caroline Logan

Georgie Logan – fifth child of Samuel and Caroline Logan

THE RILEYS

Mr. and Mrs. Riley – Riley's father and mother

Fredrick James Riley (Riley Riley) – First son of Mr. and Mrs. Riley

Laura Riley – First wife of Riley Riley

James Riley – First son of Laura and Riley

Grant Riley – Second son of Laura and Riley

Linda Jane Riley – Second wife of Riley

Brian Michael Riley – Third son of Linda Jane andRiley

Alea Nicole Newly – Step-daughter of Riley

William Victor Riley – Second son of Mr. and Mrs. Riley

OTHER FAMILY MEMBERS

Michael Nixon – Cousin – same age as Linda Jane

Winnie – Cousin – 10 years older than Linda Jane

Alexis Logan – Niece of Linda

Jade – Canine daughter of Linda and Riley

Jax – Feline son of Linda and Riley

THE FRIENDS

Gina and Marie – Roommates of Linda while in college

RaNae – Friend of Linda since grade school

Bobby – Friend of Linda

Allen – Friend of Linda and Carrot

Susan and Jim Rittenhouse – Friends and shipmate

Cheryl and Mark – Friends and shipmate

Jane – Neighbor of Linda and Riley

Lillie and Jack – Alcoholic friends and roommate of Riley after our separation

Sheila – Riley's special friend

Duncan – Linda Jane's special friend

Kenny and Joanie – Friends of Linda's

Rey – Employment supervisor and friend

Bob and Steve – Riley's roommates before coming to live with me

THE MEDICAL PROS

Dr. A – The only primary care doctor to admit he knows nothing about alcoholism

Dr. H – addictionologist who wanted to make Riley his "poster child"

Dr. G – internal medicine doctor

Dr. L – primary care doctor

Erica – physician's assistant to Dr. L

Dr. White -- Cardiologist

Janet – Visiting nurse

Tammy – Hospice nurse

GEOGRAPHICAL ROAD MAP

For Linda

OAKLAND, CA

1966   Upscale apartment – First meeting of Riley

1966   Riley's studio – Riley's first place without roommates

1967   Linda's studio – Cut expenses after job loss and discovery of pregnancy

           Linda's Aunt's house – Brian is born

           Apartment in Oakland

1969   Linda marries Peter Newly

GEORGIA

1971   Alea is born

CALIFORNIA

1971   Reconnection with Riley

VIRGINIA

1972   Village near Norfolk – First residence shared as a family

CALIFORNIA

1974   Waiting for Riley's return from deployment and transfer to Connecticut

CONNECTICUT

1975   Apartment complex – Join Riley in Connecticut

           Townhouse – Second Connecticut residence

CALIFORNIA

1978   Lease-Purchase House – Awaiting Riley's transfer orders to California

CONNECTICUT

1980   Resort house – After denied orders to California, we get married

VIRGINIA

1981   Town north of Norfolk

1983   Navy housing – Riley goes to his first rehab center

1984   Town north of Norfolk – We buy a house

1990   Apartment – after losing our house – Riley and I separate

CALIFORNIA

2000   Richard's house

2002   Crawford house

2003   St. Louis failure and return to California

              Kenny and Joanie's house – Southern California

2004   Upland house, Brian dies

2008   San Jacinto, Riley returns

NORTH CAROLINA

2009   The Hart house

2010   The Country house

INTRODUCTION

I'm in an unpleasant situation. My alcoholic husband, Riley, has exceeded any reasonable expectation of continued breathing time. He has been through the rehab process more than a dozen times. I've been told at least eight times that he will not live another six months without detox. I've also been told he will not survive detox when he was smack dab in the middle of it. After his last detox, the doctor took me aside and told me he would never survive another one. I promised Riley, I would not force him into detox again.

I anticipate and plan for the end which, unfortunately, always feels as though it would be a blessing. We have even gotten to the place of having hospice involved in his care during his final days. But his final days never arrive. In the past, I would always end up insisting he go to the emergency room, he detoxes, we are told he won't make it this time, and he recovers.

This book is about what I have found to be true during the experience of surviving my husband's alcoholism. No two drunks are the same. My experience may not be the same as anyone else. But, this book is generated from my own personal experience of living with a person who has been an alcoholic for more than 40 years. I will only attest to what has transpired over my lifetime with the alcoholic that has directly affected me. I will explain how my childhood experiences groomed me to be the perfect little homemaker and caretaker. What I write here will be bare-naked honesty.

I'm neither a counselor nor a medical professional. I have no formal education concerning alcoholism, except for the support classes offered when a family member is in rehab. Other than my personal experiences, any other information contained in this book has been learned from researching so many websites and reference materials that I could never list them all. I do, however, include a listing of helpful websites and books.

I've accumulated several years in the AA and Al-Anon communities and am very familiar with the concepts. But as my alcoholic has progressed through his addiction, I have found little comfort in 12-step support groups. In fact, many of the Al-Anon concepts are contradictory to the circumstances of an end-stage caretaker.

I'm a survivor. And surviving as a non-alcoholic in the world of alcoholic behavior is an education unto itself. I want to share my experiences and provide support to others in my situation. It is crucial that these families know that they are not alone.

I hope you can take from this book the knowledge that may be hard to get, or understand, in any other fashion.

ABSENCE OF SANITY

I woke up this morning to a beautiful sunrise. The orange hue made the tree tops appear to be silhouettes resembling black construction paper cut-outs one would find in an elementary classroom. There was a quiet peacefulness that promised a fresh new start. But, in my world, promises are never meant to be kept.

The smell of fresh coffee calls to me. The creamy, hot, dark liquid tastes just as good as it smells. I sink into the big blue overstuffed chair and enjoy watching the neighbor dog briskly scamper across the street looking for her BFF to come out and play. Anxious to join her friend, Jade whines to go out. As I open the door for her, I hear Riley make his way to the kitchen. I take a deep breath and feel my muscles stiffen. Reality is upon me. No matter how pretty the sunrise, wonderful the coffee, peaceful the morning – it is just a prelude to insanity.

Linda Bartee Doyne (aka Linda Jane Riley)

PART ONE

THE END IS THE BEGINNING

I listened closely, trying to understand what my daughter was telling me. I didn't think I heard her right. Why did the hospital call Alea? Brian was in the emergency room?? He's critical?? In intensive care?? They need what? My permission?? Why?? How?? When??

I gathered some things into a bag and broke every speed limit between my house and the hospital. A drive that normally took four hours, when made by a mother with her child in trouble, can take far less than three. I know. I did it. I crossed my fingers and hoped that my old Rosie car would not break down.

The radio stopped working months ago. I didn't need it anyway because the only sound I could hear was the prayer emanating from my mouth. "Please God help my son now! I know he is 41 years old, but he is still my baby boy." Besides the prayers, I had a lot of questions. Why did Alea call me from 3,000 miles away and not his fiancé who was only 200 miles away? Why had the hospital not called me instead of Alea? Was Tina afraid to call me? I just didn't understand the sequence of events.

The familiar landmarks clicked by. The group of houses on the ocean nestled along a curve on the highway was now in my rear-view mirror. I knew the railroad trestle was just ahead followed by the short tunnel, the windmills, the Madonna Inn and I would be there. The number on the speedometer was above the speed limit, but everything was moving so slowly.

Alea would get an emergency flight from North Carolina to Los Angeles. At first, she had wanted me to wait and meet her at LAX so we could make the trip together. But I couldn't wait another eight hours – I needed to be in San Luis Obispo right now. Every minute that I was not with Brian was a minute I would never have again.

When I walked into his room, he gave me a gigantic smile and said "Maaaw! You came! Why did you cut your hair?" I started to give him some reason, but stopped realizing that it really didn't matter. He knew I was there. I told him I loved him and that he had to get better so he could take me fishing. "I don't think I'm going to make it outta this." His statement was flat and had finality to it. I countered with an "of course you are – you're my tough guy!" But, somewhere in my heart, I knew he was probably right.

His eyes, beautiful blue eyes, were swimming in a sea of yellow and his jaundiced skin appeared as though he had not showered in a while. His beard had grown out just a little bit so there was stubble on his cheeks. His fingers were swollen and his nails were dirty. His curly blonde locks were oily and dull. This was a far cry from the handsome guy that could attract a woman from a mile away.

My first instinct was to pick him up, take him home, clean him up, and make him better. But I couldn't because he had an IV line in his arm which was connected to several bags of fluid slowly dripping into his system. He had monitors attached to him which were feeding vital information to the nurse's station. The little lines racing across the monitor in his room were doing some kind of rhythmic waltz across the screen. Up. Down. Up. Up. Down. Up. It looked normal – not like the ones that were attached to my mother during her final hospital stay. Brian must be doing OK. Because his lines were not as erratic as Mom's, I concluded that he must be doing OK. Right?

Alea arrived and we took turns making sure Brian was never left alone. I tried to get answers from his fiancé, Tina, but I didn't understand what I was hearing.

Evidently, Brian had begun drinking to the point of not being able to eat, sleep or function in a day to day manner. When Tina woke up that morning, Brian was in the bathroom being sick. By the time she left for work, he was sitting on the sofa with a bowl between his feet. He was vomiting blood. He was pale and almost non-responsive. She left for work. I listened to her as she explained how my only son ended up in intensive care.

I was confused… she left him and went to work when she knew he was vomiting blood?? Are you sure about that?? I can't imagine leaving someone I love in that state and just blithely going off and leaving him alone for the day. Did she not understand the severity of the situation?

After being gone for five hours, she returned for lunch at 1 p.m. to find him still sitting in the same position and still mostly unresponsive. When he did respond he was rude and cantankerous. She had had enough and called 911.

It's a small town where everyone knows everyone else. Sometimes they would bend the rules if it helped whoever they were trying to assist. Even if Brian resisted, he would be going to the hospital today – right then. It was an effort, but the EMT's got him down the three flights of stairs and into the ambulance. He was still vomiting blood and passing out.

In the emergency room, they started pumping him with fluids and he started to regain some consciousness. Once he was stabilized, they transferred him to the ICU. That's when I got there. The doctors met with me and Alea and explained that Brian may not make it through this detox period. They needed to go in and repair the bleeding in his stomach using some sort of clamps that would be placed around the bleeders. The hard part was that the doctors didn't know if he would regain consciousness after the surgery. If the bleeding wasn't stopped, he would bleed to death. If he had the surgery, he may never regain consciousness – isn't that called "dead?" Neither option sounded acceptable, but we agreed to the surgery and crossed our fingers.

We spent the time getting a motel room. We needed a base where we could shower, nap and meet with other family members.

The phone call came that Brian was out of surgery. We were encouraged when he not only made it through, but woke up and told all of us that he loved us. He thanked us for being there. We made general conversation. He asked for some Captain Morgan and a cigarette. Alea told him she would go get him a cigarette, but she'd have to pass on the rum. She had no intention of getting his smokes, but it quieted him for a few minutes.

We stayed with him constantly, taking turns to nap and eat. The brother and sister, who had spent their entire lives being extremely close, bantered back and forth. I could see the fear in her eyes as his arguments and teasing became less and less. He was drifting in and out of knowing where he was and what he was doing. When he thought they were on a fishing boat, Alea played along.

By this time, we had made all the necessary phone calls to all the relatives. Our clan was already joining forces. We were famous for that. Don't mess with us because as a group we are a unit to be reckoned with. It seemed no sooner had the calls been made that relatives were showing up. It was almost as if we thought our banning together could change Brian's condition. It didn't, but during the times when he was cognizant, he appreciated seeing each of them.

My mind went back to a time when Brian was only a toddler. Carrot, my best friend turned sister-in-law, had a son, Len, just 8 months older than Brain. We interchanged the kids all the time. She ended up with four and I had my two. They were stair steps in age and they all were treated as siblings.

We shared the same pediatrician who dubbed us as the "interchangeable mothers." He never knew which Mom would bring which kid into his office. And he never questioned our authority to give permission for treatment. This was the same doctor who cared for my own little brothers. He knew our family well.

They would all be here… Carrot and all of her four kids along with their significant others. My little brother's kids would also be here, at least the ones who could get here. We were also joined by Tina's son, James, and all Brian's SLO (San Luis Obispo) friends. We made a formidable group. There was strength in our numbers.

Riley called to let me know that he had arrived with his friend, Sheila. They would be at the motel, if we needed him. He was drunk, she was drunk, his son was dying and he was there having a fling with this chick. I hated them both that day. What I needed was for him to be sober and supportive. In reality, I knew it would not happen, but I was still hoping.

When Riley and Sheila finally arrived at the hospital, they brought a bottle of vodka with them for Brian. We didn't discover this until after they had left. During the visit, they were instructed to only touch Brian very gently because anything more would start bleeding just under the skin. When I looked in on Riley and Sheila, I found her giving him a massage. I told her to stop, but she just looked at me slurring that it would be OK, it would make him feel better. I told her to stop or get out. They left and returned to the motel room. We did not see them again for two days.

Brian was enjoying having his sister and other "siblings" surround him in his room. And the fact that Brian really didn't understand what was going on, where he was, or who he was talking to, didn't really matter. They talked, laughed and, when Brian could not see, they cried. I loved seeing them all together. But I hated the reason why.

As Brian slipped farther and farther from us, we took turns sitting at his bedside. He was not left alone even for a minute because he might wake up and feel abandoned.

Gradually, Brian stopped responding altogether. It was a slow descent and we kept trying to get him back. We called his name and smoothed his hair. He was given sponge baths, which he loved, but he did not once make mention of our actions. He just kept his eyes closed and seemed to be sleeping.

He wasn't sleeping. He had drifted into a coma. All our prodding and pleading, joking and teasing, couldn't make him respond. It wouldn't have been so bad if he had looked as though he was getting some well-earned sleep which included pleasant dreams. But there was no peaceful expression on his face. He just seemed devoid of anything.

The time had come for a major decision to be made. I tried to wait for Riley to appear so he could be a part of that decision. I included Brian's fiancé, Tina, but, in the end, the decision was mine. We terminated his feeding tube, took away his life support and gave him only morphine so he would not be in pain. They moved him to another wing in a giant sized room where the family could all be with him at the same time.

I felt like a zombie set to "react" mode. We were all praying for a change in his condition that would keep him on this planet. I knew Brian believed in God and I tried to find a minister who would come to the hospital to support us. It took a while, but finally one showed up and offered to stay with us and help us through. My niece's boyfriend prayed with me for a miracle. We prayed for

17

guidance. We prayed for a peaceful passing. And I prayed that this was all just a bad dream that would culminate in a happy ending. I didn't want to be in reality.

After days of being comatose, Brian opened his beautiful baby blues and looked up with a big smile. He took a deep breath and then left us forever. The only prayer that God answered was the one about a peaceful passing. My only son... my loving, handsome, baby boy went to heaven where he could join his grandparents and uncles and all those who passed before. He was now where he could watch over us all. He must have been devastated to see how much pain we were in.

I listened as the doctor explained what he thinks happened. At one time Brian was doing a lot of world-wide travelling for his job. One of his jobs took him to Hong Kong and another to Columbia. It is most likely that he contracted some type of liver ailment during his travels. It may never have caused him any real physical problems. Brian was never one for going to the doctor or complaining about aches and pains. But, for some reason, he had stepped up his alcohol consumption over the past few years and his weakened liver could not handle the increase. I had not seen him for more than a year. Although I had concerns for his love of Captain Morgan, I had no idea his drinking had turned into end-stage alcoholism. It appeared that he went from zero to sixty in about two years ending in his death.

I was exhausted. The sobbing hit me uncontrollably over and over again. We made arrangements and turned my baby into dust. How could this have happened? The feeling of helplessness and guilt overwhelmed me. If I had just known. I saw the signs, but his fiancé never conveyed to me how bad things really were. Whenever I was on the phone, she always hid out in the bathroom refusing to talk to either me or Alea. I made other excuses, why had she left for work when he was vomiting blood? If she had just gotten him to the hospital sooner, if I had just visited more often... if... if... if... Why had I not given him enough protection? And the big one -- what kind of mother signs papers to terminate her child's life? I allowed my little boy to die. I wanted to die. If I had been left alone long enough, I could have done it.

The family focus switched from Brian to me. Carrot and the kids surrounded me, watched me, loved me. And I didn't die because they would not ever allow that to happen. From the moment of her arrival, Carrot did not leave my side. She held me up while Len, the closest thing to a brother Brian had, held Alea up. Their efforts were strengthened by the sheer numbers of our family. All of my nieces and nephews were there for us. They were our rocks. Without them we would have been doomed to wander around in a dazed state of mind, aimlessly wandering the streets of San Luis Obispo. They didn't leave us until we insisted that they go to our hometown and start making arrangements for a memorial service.

Riley showed up at the service. His roommates had cleaned him up and made him presentable. He did not bring Sheila, nor did he join the family for the reception afterwards. He went back home and crawled back into the vodka bottle where he was comfortable.

We all returned to our homes. Alea went back to North Carolina and I went back to San Bernardino County. I went through the motions of returning to normal when I was visible. But, my insides were a liquid puddle of misery. When no one was looking, I just wanted to die.

They (whoever "they" are) say it will get better. The pain will get easier to bear. You will come through this. And the worst one of all... he is at peace and is no longer in pain. Don't believe it for a nano-second. It's been two years and it doesn't get any easier to look at his picture. The pain is with me every day. Telling me he's at peace doesn't help me – how do they know? Did they ask him? Of course not. He can't answer BECAUSE HE'S DEAD!!

No matter how much I rationalize, no matter who I blame, I know that I failed my son. I did not protect him. I don't care how old he was. I don't care that he made his own decisions. I am guilty of ignoring a problem that I didn't want to see. If I could prevent Riley from dying of this horrible thing called alcoholism, why could I not save my baby. I should be, and am, ashamed of myself.

Things do, however, get back to a new definition of normal. There's something missing, but it is as normal as it can get. I started working again. I started seeing my friends again. I began living again.

A Special Gift
(Blog Post, A Special Gift, 2/21/11)

Although my son didn't live all that far from me – only about a 4 hour drive – I really didn't see him very often. He and Tina were always working and she seldom wanted to make that trip. My transportation was "iffy" and I didn't want to push my car to make the journey. But we talked every weekend and often during the week. I seldom talked to Tina for any more than a "hi" and "good-by". Whenever Brian forced her to talk to us, she was distant. It was as though she was holding back and now I know that she was doing exactly that – holding back.

I loved Tina and treated her twin boys, James and John as though they were my own grandsons. They were a part of my family. Why had she not been honest and open with me?? I had always supported Brian's relationship with her. She had nothing to fear from me. However, there is a history. Her father is a recovering alcoholic, and I suspect that she is probably an alcoholic. I ignored those signs. She was highly functional and seemed to be handling the oars in the boat very well. But, in the end, it seemed I had unwittingly placed a high level of expectations upon someone who was neither capable nor desirous of meeting them. I did not realize that my expectations were unrealistic.

You would have thought I would have known what was going on, but I didn't. There were innuendos and comments, but nothing concrete. I talked with Brian often about his drinking and asked what I thought were all the right questions, but I was not listening close enough.

The point is, I failed my son. As a mother I failed to protect him because I didn't realize that he was in danger. I have beat myself up over this so many times and I try to rationalize and give myself a break. There are no breaks for me, my inaction killed my son. So I grieve every day for my little boy who never really grew up. He may have been an adult, but for me he was still my baby boy. For him I ask, why? What if? But I know the answer and I do NOT like it.

There is another side to this. There is Riley, the father of my little boy who shared the same addiction to alcohol. He has been saved many times, from a path of his own choosing, which complicates the lives of everyone around him.

Riley and I had a discussion once about his (Riley's) death when the time comes. He is not drinking at this moment and therefore is not in eminent danger of dying. But, it is just a matter of time before the cycle begins again and he will meet his demise. And, in my jaded mind, his death will be the ultimate gift to me, Alea and Alea's son, Ryan, because it will be the gift of freedom from insanity. We have already grieved for the husband, father and grandfather that we knew in the past. It has taken us years to get to this point. But, here we are. When he dies our tears will be representative of the joy of being able to let go. We will miss the Riley we knew before he became end-stage, but we've been missing him for a very long time already.

So why is it different for Brian? I never had the opportunity to accept the reality of his addiction. I never detached because I didn't have the conflict with Brian that I have had with Riley. Brian never lived in my house as an alcoholic. He never caused me to be concerned. He never went to a rehab center. I never detached because I didn't know I needed to. And so I am left with this immense hole in my heart.

It seems cavalier of me to say, "Detach and you will not be in so much pain." Or, "Just do as I say and everything will be rosey." Well… guess what? It is NOT rosey and will never BE rosey. The loss of a loved one hurts even on a good day in a bad relationship. But the loss can be less intense if you can see it for what it is, a gift.

My son gave me a gift – even if I didn't want it, he gave me the gift of not watching him follow in his father's footsteps. He gave me the gift of not consuming my life with insanity. He gave me the gift of forcing me to let him go. If I don't believe his death is a gift, I am doomed to live in the darkness of his absence, grieving every day for the loss of my sweet baby boy.

Alcoholism is a terminal disease. If you don't believe it's a disease, then it's a terminal situation. No matter how you look at it there are only two ways out, sobriety or death. For most of us non-alcoholics, we realize that fact and fight it every single day. Even when we say we don't — we still do. When the prospect of sobriety fades, the grim reaper lives at the front door waiting to give the non-alcoholic a package wrapped in bright, happy paper.

Riley and Mr. Reaper will give me a gift, a welcomed one. He will give me the gift of sanity. He is not ready yet to wrap it up with a pretty bow, but eventually he will hand it to me. I will gladly accept his gift of setting me free from his alcoholic insanity.

SO NOW WHAT?

Tina moved on. Within a year of Brian's death she filled the void with another man. From my understanding, he is also an alcoholic. I have no idea what happened to the boys. Well, they were actually young men when Brian died. I have missed them, James especially. I have worried about the path they may be taking and have often wished I could divert them from the mistakes of Brian and Tina. But, I do accept the things I cannot change. I received an e-mail sometime during the past year from Tina letting me know that her new man won the lottery and she was now sitting in high cotton. I don't know what she was trying to accomplish by sending it to me. Maybe she was getting the message across that her life was better without Brian. I don't know. Well... good for her...

With the loss of Brian, I felt a pressing need to be there for Alea and to protect her and help her have the fullest, happiest life she could possibly have. Alea and her family had to be my focus now. I knew she needed me. We needed each other. Recovering from Brian's death was no easier for her than it was for me. She isn't one to let all her emotions show all the time. But, I knew... I knew she was struggling. I needed to forget my self-loathing and focus on the one child I had left.

The 3,000 miles separating us was becoming a difficult obstacle to overcome. Within a month, I decided that I would save all the money I could. I moved to a small cottage owned by a friend and save more than a $1K a month on rent. The plan was for me to move to North Carolina just before Christmas of the following year. We had a plan and it was a good one.

The cottage was just a small one-bedroom, but it had a private fenced back yard and everything I really needed on a daily basis. Since it was owned by a friend, I took some liberties on making a few improvements which worked to suit my needs. I liked it there. It was comfortable, not very quiet but I solved that by turning on the air conditioner and/or playing the stereo or television.

HOW I GOT HERE

Another couple of months went by before I received a phone call from Riley's roommates. One of the roommates was a circuit court judge and, although he was surviving MS and lived his days with the aid of an assistant, he was still sitting the bench. I liked him. He was always friendly to me. It was the assistant who actually called. If I did not get Riley out of his house, they would have him committed as a danger to himself and others.

My first thought – so what??? Why should I care what happens to him? He's dug his hole and made his choices. I wanted nothing to do with him. They needed an answer within a couple of days.

What I didn't know was that Alea had called to talk to her father. But, she got the assistant instead. He told her what was going on and she said she would hop on a flight in the morning and come get him. Her next call was to me to tell me she was taking her father back to North Carolina so he could live with her and her husband.

At that time, Alea also had her son, pregnant daughter-in-law and granddaughter living in her two bed, one bath, home. I don't know where she thought she would put her father – maybe from a hook in the hallway. Alea's response when I protested was that the kids would only be there for a few months.

I had been beating myself up over not protecting Brian. There was no way in hell I would allow her to ruin her life or her marriage by adding her drunken father into her home. I immediately called the roommates and told them I would come get him. Alea did not have a say in this. Riley and I were still legally married and the decision was mine and mine alone.

I knew it would be a challenge. Riley's drinking had always been a challenge. He was mentally, subliminally abusive and had had no respect for me or our marriage. I became happier in my life the moment I left him. In order to leave, I lost a lot – my house, my car and most of the personal possessions that I valued. But those things were not as important as getting away from the insanity that he created. My kids were grown and out of the house – it was just me – I had nothing to lose. After 20 years, I was removing myself from the center of his alcoholic circle.

We lived happily apart for almost 15 years. Because he was retired military, there would be no divorce. I felt that I had given him good years of my life while dealing with the military, womanizing and drinking. I supported his career and even served as ombudsman for several of his commands. I had earned my military benefits and was not about to risk losing them.

After separating, Riley went through several rehab centers – I think there were 13 rehab centers and he went through detox at least a half-dozen times. The last three detox situations were extremely traumatic for the family. We were told that he would surely not survive. I was left to comfort my children who were already grieving from the anticipated loss of their father. I watched them suffer and hoped for a quick ending. But the end did not come. He survived only to return to drinking almost immediately following discharge. The family was left in shock as the process was repeated, over and over again.

And now… now… he was coming back to my house. According to his roommates, he was near death. But, I'd seen that before and he was still alive. Sometimes I thought he must be immortal.

THE PLAN

My plan was only to give him a safe and soft place to die. There seemed to be no sense in trying to convince him to stop drinking. Been there and done that so many times, a repetition just didn't seem logical. So I was just going to let him go. Let the alcoholic come to its inevitable final conclusion.

Well, that was the plan…

THE FLAW

The First Law of Robotics: *A robot cannot cause the harm of a human or through inaction allow a human to come to harm.*

In order to adhere to the plan I had to no longer view this alcoholic as a human being or remember that he is the father of my children or a person that I once loved and would lie down my life to protect. I had view this person as one who is not deserving of medical attention and/or any attempt at preserving his physical life.

I didn't know how to do what I felt I must do in order to fulfill the plan because to not care about a human life; to not make every attempt at prolonging or saving a life; feels somehow immoral. Although I'm not the epitome of virtue, I just didn't think I could, in essence cause a person's death by reason of non-action. For some reason, I felt I must adhere to the first law of robotics.

Maybe I'm not really a human, maybe I'm a robot that was built specifically for this alcoholic. Was there something my parents had neglected to tell me??

PART TWO

FAMILY VALUES

Family values are ideas, traditions, and morals that are handed down to each of us from our parents, their parents, and so on through the generations. These values dictate how a family functions inside the unit. During the process of a child's mental and emotional growth, he/she learns the basic ways of how to live their life and how to raise their children by the things they learn within their family. I grew up abiding by Sam and Caroline Logan Family Values.

OPPOSITES ATTRACT

My parents, Sam and Caroline, were from directly opposing backgrounds – a farm boy and the socialite -- a direct instance of opposites attracting. My mother let my father believe he was the head of the household and that worked for them. Including me, my family consisted of five children born to my parents and numerous cousins who lived with us at one time or another. We seldom had less than ten mouths to feed at the dinner table.

My father was tall, sturdy and handsome with his blonde wavy hair and steel blue eyes. He had a wide mischievous smile and a deep hearty laugh. He came from a long line of country farmers who had settled in the heart of Texas. Their ancestors had come from Georgia, North and South Carolina, and Virginia. Some were farmers others were businessmen, noblemen, plantation owners and explorers such as Lewis Meriwether of The Lewis and Clark Expedition fame. The Logan's and their ancestors fought on both sides of the Revolutionary and Civil Wars and proudly defended our country in World Wars I and II, as well as the Korean and Viet Nam conflicts. These people were patriots and our country's leaders, but in the mix there were also horse thieves, kidnappers, rabble rousers, and trouble-makers. They were an eclectic group, indeed.

Caroline Jane Evans was petite standing only 5'2" with her shoes on and her back stretched. She had ash blonde hair and blue/green eyes. She had dainty hands and feet and people often mistook her for a weakling. They would be wrong. She had firm values and opinions which she expressed freely – and often.

She was the daughter of a small family who immigrated to the United States from Germany sometime around the 1800's. Information doesn't seem to flow so freely from her side of the family. I know my grandfather was an architectural engineer who designed the new super highways that traversed through the upper Midwest states. My grandmother was a woman's tailor. The family was not rich, but they were considered to be upper class in economic and social status.

My mother met my father while he was serving in the Army during World War II. It was almost love at first sight and when the war was over, my parents married. The Logan clan had relocated to the San Francisco Bay Area and my mother moved there to start her new life.

It had to have been difficult for my prim and proper mother to come from a home where she shared a bathroom with only one person to a house where there was NO bathroom at all. The lifestyle was very different for her and the adjustment must have been incredibly hard. But, my mother was a woman who stood by her commitments and combined with the fact that she was deeply in love, she made the necessary tweaks to her expectations in order to have a life with my father. She was no longer an Evan, she was now a Logan.

It was huge thing to be a Logan. It was a giant-sized family and there were lots of things that my mother had to come to accept. Meals were all eaten around a huge dining table that easily sat twelve people. Grocery money was combined and was purchased as a group led by my paternal grandmother. There was a family garden and chickens. Hand-down clothing was exchanged throughout the family and new dresses were a rarity. Children were exchanged between houses like cups of sugar from a neighbor. Each adult was allowed and expected to disciple any child who misbehaved at any time. My mother was not married just to my father, but rather to the entire Logan family.

A FRESH BEGINNING

Eventually my mother's Evans Family Trust became available to her and she purchased some land away from the Logan complex where she and my father could build a home of their own. My father bartered marine construction work for architectural plans for the new home. My mother paid for the materials and the shell of our home was erected. Both of my parents and my uncles closed in the walls and did the finish work.

The new house had not just one bathroom, but two bathrooms. There was hot and cold running water in the kitchen, a fireplace and a formal dining room. The balance of my mother's money was spent on new furnishings. I had my own bedroom which was right across the hall from the front bathroom. I was five years old and in first grade when we moved into the new house.

It was a landmark in my mother's life when we moved into our family home. We now ate meals in our own kitchen and they were prepared from food my mother had shopped for without the accompaniment of my grandmother. I didn't share my bath water with either of my two brothers. And there were no bunk beds which meant no pee dripping down on me in the middle of the night. My mother was now the queen of her kingdom and I was a happy princess.

WHO NEEDS FRIENDS

The Logan's were still a formidable force as a unit. We were always together at holidays, weddings, funerals and often on weekends. Each summer the kids were sent to spend a week or two at some other family member's home. I remember when I was upset about having no real friends come to visit at home. My father's response was that I didn't need friends because I had family. In his mind that was all that I needed.

In my house, teasing was a way of life. I wasn't very good at it, so I stopped trying to keep up and just gave up. I was the only girl child in a household of testosterone. I was in the minority and my words often got lost in the chaotic male banter. In today's terms, I suppose, you could say that I was bullied by my male counterparts. Back then, it was just something I had to accept. When I would complain to either of my parents, I was told that they do that because they love me. So... I assumed that this is what love looks like. I wasn't so sure I wanted any part of it.

I always knew my place in the scheme of things. The boys always went with my father and uncles to work on the dredges, pile drivers, cranes and tug boats. I stayed home and cleaned the house, did their laundry and changed their bed linens. I picked up their dirty underwear from behind the bathroom door and washed their whiskers and soap scum from the sinks. I helped prepare their dinner. In the summer, I worked in the garden and helped Mom keep up with the office tasks. My place was in the home. My duty was to make the males warm, happy, and comfortable. Whenever I asked to go along with the boys the answer was always the same – we all work and my job was in the house. The waterfront was no place for a girl.

GET OFF MY PORCH

When I was in sixth grade my grandmother became very ill and could no longer live alone. My mother was pregnant with my younger brother, Evan, but she welcomed my grandmother into our home agreeing to take care of the ailing woman whom she had grown to love as a mother.

Grandma was average height and was a bit overweight, but not obese. Her hands and face was wrinkled from hard work in the sun. She was strong and could work in the garden for hours and then cook a meal from the vegetables she harvested. She smiled a lot making her blue eyes twinkle.

I thought my grandmother was about the bravest woman I had ever known. I had listened to her stories of life on the farm in Texas and was fascinated at what I learned. I sat next to her and watched as she stitched homemade bonnets on her treadle sewing machine. She was resourceful and I admired how she made my mother stop the car so she could get out and pick the mustard greens along the highway. She wasted nothing and considered herself to be rich beyond measure.

When Grandma came to stay with us, my own bed was moved across the floor to the other side of my bedroom. A hospital bed was situated across the room from my bed. The bed would become my grandmother's primary existence for as long as she was sick. My Aunt Katie took time from being a Navy nurse and provided instruction on how to care for Grandma. We learned how to give and remove the bedpan and how to give her the correct dosages of medication. We practiced on how to administer shots by using oranges. And a bell was installed that would ring next to my mother's bed if Grandma needed her in the middle of the night.

Grandma did her very best not to be a burden. She was insightful and intuitive about my mother and all her babies that lived in that house. This was a very uncomfortable pregnancy for my mother. She had around the clock morning sickness. Caring for Grandma was no easy task.

I was not a little girl anymore. One of my aunts made it clear to me that I should do as much as I could for Grandma to take the load off my mother's shoulders. One aunt went as far to tell me that to do anything else would be paramount to laziness which was not a Logan trait. I felt ashamed that I had not done more to that point.

Usually, Grandma would wake me up in the middle of the night and ask for the bed pan and I complied. As soon as I got home from school, I would make her a snack which we would share while talking about my day. I thought I was helping, evidently I wasn't helping enough. I began taking a more active role by giving her shots and sponge baths. I would read to her and clean up her meal trays. I did not want to be lazy and I definitely needed to prove that I was a Logan.

By the time I reached eighth grade, one of my aunts bought a house down the street from us and moved Grandma in with her. I still took care of her. Every weekend I went to Grandmas and stayed with her while my aunt went to the city to work in a beauty salon. Friday night through Monday morning, I was Grandmas constant companion. I didn't mind that I didn't get to be with the few friends that I had. I was doing what was important – I was caretaking my grandmother.

One Saturday evening, Grandma was hallucinating after being prescribed a new drug. She managed to use her walker and get herself to the living room. She whispered to me to hand her that gun while pointing to the broom. I had been warned that she could show signs of confusion and I went along with her request. She snatched the broom from me and pointed it toward the front door.

"You better git outta here!!" she screamed. "Git on down the road and leave usin's alone!! I've got a big ole shotgun here. I know how ta use it and I'll blow a hole rit thu ya!! Ya all just git off my porch!" She ranted on and on about getting off her porch and made me stand behind her as she continued in her protective mindset.

"Grandma, should I call the sherrif?" I asked – her response was – NO – she could handle this. I listened closely trying to share the sounds she was hearing, but I came up with nothing. After a while she calmed down and told me everything was OK. She asked me to help her get back to bed. Once she was settled back between her covers, I called my father and he came down to the house.

Grandma liked to sit on the porch and watch me sweep it clean each day when I was with her. I always encouraged her because I told her I could not sweep the porch unless she watched for places I was missing. We had the cleanest porch in town. The night my father came to the house after Grandma's shotgun episode, he asked me if I had sweep the porch that evening. I told him yes and he said Grandma must have heard whoever had dropped all those potato chips on the porch.

By the winter of my ninth grade year, Grandma died. I was traumatized by the loss. I had never felt anything so painful in my life. There was a hole that couldn't be filled. All of her babies had been summoned to her bedside along with my aunts and uncles. We were to say goodbye. Grandma took my hand and told me she loved me and that I was special from the rest. She told me I would be a strong woman and keep 'em off the porch. I remember feeling as though I couldn't breathe as I walked from her room. Tears were streaming down my face and I couldn't see. There was no one there to guide me. No one took my hand or held me close. Everyone was busy in the room as my grandmother passed into a world where I could not go. I knew I would never be the same.

DID I TELL YOU?
MY NAME IS CARETAKER

It was September 1965 and school had just begun. The days were still warm and the evenings were cool. There was still a slow and easy pace about town. My father needed to pick up a part for some piece of equipment or something and asked if I'd like to ride along. The trip would take about an hour each way. Sure, I'd love to have some one-on-one time with him.

On the same day, my mother needed to get a part for her washing machine. She had been up all night with my youngest brother, Georgie, who had been vomiting. My oldest brother, Richard, had left his brand new Mustang for her to drive to the parts house. As much as she needed the washing machine to be fixed, she was just too tired to drive.

My cousin, Michael, who was only a few days older than me, was staying with us for his last year of high school. He volunteered to run the errand for my mother. Not knowing how Richard would feel about someone else driving the Mustang, Mom was hesitant. Michael seemed to get into trouble easier than the rest of the kids and she was thinking about that. What if he didn't come straight home?

Michael reassured my mother that it would be a straight shot there and back. In fact, Evan and Charlie could ride with him if it made her feel better. The younger, grade school age boys would make it more difficult for Michael to run amok so she relented.

Daddy and I were driving through town on our way back from the city. Abiding the 20 mph speed limit laws, my father made his way up Main Street to Second Avenue where he followed the highway by making the obligatory left turn. The city park was on our right. Someone pulled up close behind us and flashed his lights, then honked his horn. Daddy pulled over and the other car came up next to us.

It was Ben, a family friend, who yelled out his window to my father. "Caroline was in an accident out near Sandy Ridge Road. She's in pretty bad shape. Better go straight to the hospital." My father thanked him and drove on. I have no idea how, but my father managed to get us home.

We didn't expect anyone to be in the house when we walked in, but my mother was there. She was walking around the house with Georgie in her arms.

"You're OK??" Daddy asked. "Ben told there had been an accident. He said you were hurt." Georgie was pushed into my arms and my mother went pale.

"It has to be Michael, Evan and Charlie!! Ben must have thought I was in the car! If they've been in an accident, where are they??" The tears were coming now. My father was on the phone calling the police department just as a cop car pulled into our driveway.

The boys had been taken to a county hospital because the local hospital didn't have the facilities to care for their extensive injuries. Momma was crying. Daddy's big hand was wiping his face in a downward motion from forehead to chin. Georgie was crying. I stood there like a zombie. I bounced Georgie up and down trying to get him to stop crying. My parents said nothing to me. They got in the car and drove off. I surmised they were going to the hospital.

The living room seemed like a vast open room without any hiding places. I didn't know when Georgie had gotten his last bottle or his last dose of Tylenol. I focused on him. Change the diaper. Give him a bottle. Put a dropper of Tylenol in his mouth. Rock him gently. He calmed down and fell asleep.

Richard and my other cousins had been working all day. They would be hungry when they got home. I started preparing dinner. I did not cry. I was not sad. I was scared because I had no idea of what was going on. But, dinner needed to be fixed. People would be hungry and it was up to me to feed them.

I was just about done with dinner when my older cousin, Winnie, walked through the door with her two little boys. I asked her if she knew anything and she told me "Not yet." The rest of the guys filed in and we gave them the news. They ate and left for the hospital.

My boyfriend, Bobby called. I finally started crying. I knew nothing. No one had told me anything. Could he come over? Yes. He'd be right there.

Winnie stayed with Georgie and I promised to call her with any news I got. Bobby and I went to the hospital. My father pulled me aside in the waiting room.

"Both boys look very bad. Charlie looks the worst, but really it's Evan that is most in trouble. It will be shocking to see them, but you can't show that. Your mother needs to you to be calm and not upset. She can't help you now. She has to focus on the boys." I promised I would not upset my mother and was allowed into the room.

They were so fragile. So pale. Charlie had a cast from his waist to the big toe of his left leg. The leg was raised by a pulley. He had bags of fluid running to his arms and a mask over his face. Almost his entire face was bandaged. He looked like a sleeping mummy.

I tuned my attention to Evan, who as a newborn was so tiny that he slept in my doll's bed. He seemed tiny again. He was tightly tucked in all around his body with his arms on top of the covers. There was a large hose somehow attached to his nose. A machine was pumping air into his lungs. Identical bags of fluid were being given to him.

Both boys were cut and mangled over every exposed piece of flesh. I could not imagine what pain they must have been in. I wanted to faint, but Bobby held me up.

The boys were not expected to make it through the night. Relatives were being called from all over the country and were flying in from various airports. No one wanted to leave the hospital so Bobby volunteered to be our taxi driver.

I had things I had to do. I accompanied the insurance adjuster to view the totaled Mustang. It still had pieces of Charlie's scalp hanging onto the jagged edges of the glass spears that used to be the windshield. The gear shifter was twisted and resting in the passenger seat. The front passenger seat back was sitting sideways across the seat. The steering wheel was hanging loosely from the column. The white interior was marred with streaks of my brothers' blood. My stomach turned and I vomited before I got back into the adjusters car.

My father had his own problems adjusting to the near loss of his male off-spring. He handed me a brown grocery bag and told me I had to wash the contents. I didn't think much about it and placed it on top of the washer. Days later, I looked inside the bag and found the clothes that had been cut from the boys bodies. They were hard where the blood had dried into the folds. Bits of glass fell from them as I held them up. There was nothing left except shreds of cloth that once was a shirt or a pair of pants. I put everything back in the bag and took it out to the burn barrel. "Please, God, give me the strength to lie to my father if he asks about these clothes." I struck a match and the flames cleansed the evil from the bag. God must have heard me because my father never asked about the clothing.

Over the next few weeks the boys were taken off the danger list, my mother moved into a small apartment next door to the hospital, and I became the woman of the house. At least once a week, one of my aunts and Winnie would come by to see if there was anything they could do. But, I had it under control. I developed a routine.

Up at 5am to fix breakfast for everyone before they left for work; Get Georgie ready for Winnie to pick him up; Get ready and go to school; Winnie picks me up after school and brings Georgie and I home; Clean up around the house; Give Georgie a bottle; Prepare dinner; Clean up the dinner mess; Do some homework while Daddy gives Georgie a bath and gets him ready for bed; Rock Georgie to sleep with his bedtime bottle; Lay out my clothes; Get some sleep and start over the next day.

Dates with Bobby consisted of visits to the hospital to see the boys and my mother. It was painful to see them and painful to think about how my relationship with Bobby was changing. I loved this man. I HAD to love this man. He had been "there" for me. But, I didn't feel the driving passion or anticipation of taking the next step. It just was that I loved him and that was all.

I finally found out what had happened during that trip to get the washing machine part. Michael fell asleep and ran a stop sign ramming head on with an oncoming car. The other driver was killed instantly. Charlie was in the center of the back seat. He was thrown from the seat, hitting his left leg while breaking off the gear shifter, then through the windshield tearing off the skin on his face down to the skull, and then back through the windshield further removing the skin, and, again catching his leg on the gear shifter. He had multiple compound fractures of his left tibia. His facial skin and scalp had to be grafted back onto his head. Although his injuries were mostly external, it would take years of physical therapy and plastic surgery for him to ever have a normal life again. He would not be home any time soon.

Evan was thrown from the car and his body dragged along the road. He had massive head injuries, damage to his eyes, and internal bleeding. Although his injuries were more life threatening than his brother's, if he recovered from the first few days, he would recover completely in a much shorter time than Charlie. He would be home in about six weeks.

I was livid with Michael. I knew he had been partying the night before. I was livid with myself for not telling my parents that he had been drinking. I was livid with Michael's mother because it seemed she just wanted us all to be worried about Michael's recovery without much concern for my brothers or the dead driver. I wish I could have said that I was worried about my cousin, but in the mind of a sister about to lose her brothers – I really didn't care what happened to Michael. He deserved any bad thing that was about to take place.

After a bit more than month, Evan was released and came home. His eyesight was damaged and he would need to wear glasses. But that was the extent of his injuries.

Charlie was in the hospital for almost a whole school year. His leg was in traction and he needed extensive plastic surgery for the deep scaring of the skin that had been pulled back up over his face and skull. He would spend years in getting surgeries. As he approached adulthood, he finally told my parents that he didn't want any more. The scars had become a part of his persona. He was alive and well and didn't mind the scars. One of his legs was longer than the other and that caused him to walk with a little limp that was almost undetectable.

Everything in my life changed in those weeks after the accident. I learned a lot and I lost a lot. I wasn't an innocent young girl anymore. I was the strong woman that Grandma had said I would be. Things at school seemed to be trivial, but I immersed myself in class work. I became an excellent student. I couldn't be bothered with school friends.

CARROT AND ALLEN

I met Carrot in my mechanical drawing class and we were instant kindred spirits. In her previous school she was a mover and shaker, but at my school she was more of a loner. She was the older of two children and had had many step-fathers. We use to play around about which last name she would use this week. I knew Carrot had experienced some truly horrible things in her childhood past. She didn't share all of it with me, but I knew at some time she would. It didn't matter. She was my very best friend.

Brown curly hair framed her creamy white face. Glasses covered her blue eyes. She had a small frame, but not delicate. She was warm and friendly and could make me laugh at absolutely nothing.

Carrot lived in a trailer park located inside a resort on the river. Time spent with her at her place usually meant floating down the river in an inner tube, water skiing, sunning out on the dock, and going to Scout Hall in town for dancing. Her mother worked at the restaurant at the marina and we got plenty of hamburgers, fries and milk shakes.

Chuck was about to become her next step-father and she was about to get a new step-brother who was extremely off the cute-meter charts. With Allen's blonde hair and blue eyes, he looked like he could have starred in a surfer movie as a stand-in for Troy Donohue. He was just flippin' gorgeous. He was also kind and sweet and – he liked ME.

I met Allen during Spring Break. I had taken a live-in baby-sitting job for a family who had a river front house just past the marina. Allen was there helping his father in the machine shop. Carrot had a crush on him, but she was already dating my brother Richard. So, I figured he was fair game.

He asked me out to one of the dances and after that we were together the entire break. We took long walks down the levee. He watched television with the kids. We ate at the marina restaurant. We double dated with Richard and Carrot. We had fun. It was free and easy. We liked each other without strings attached.

When break was over, we returned to our respective worlds. For him it was college and his part time job at the bowling alley. For me it was school.

I don't know why the graduation ceremony hit me so hard. I was an emotional wreck. I kept it in check until the graduates that were in the choir took their places on the risers to sing their final songs. As I stood there waiting for my cues, a childhood friend was behind me and took my hand. I burst into tears. I felt that I would not see her again for a long time. I would probably not sing in a choir ever again. I looked around me at all the other seniors and I knew I would probably never see any of them ever again.

These people that I had been with since grade school would go their own ways, create their own worlds, and make their own futures. Most would go to a university. That wasn't even a possibility for me. Some would go into the military. Again, no possibility of that for me. I didn't know what I was going to do. All I knew was just what I would NOT be able to do.

Well... if you don't know what to do... don't do anything. The resort family asked me back to baby-sit over the summer. I didn't realize that I was being a nanny. We didn't call it that back then – it was just a live-in baby-sitting, housekeeping job. I took it and I knew I would be seeing Carrot every day. This would work for the summer. I'd figure everything out while I was there.

Just before lunch the next day, Allen went to the restaurant to get us some hamburgers. He returned with the burgers, fries and sodas for all. My mouth was watering I was so hungry. I took a bite and looked up at Allen, who had also taken a bite. We looked at each other – RAW!! The hamburgers were raw, the fries were raw and the sodas were flat.

"Who made these?" I asked.

"Carrot." He answered.

OH!! It was so very clear. Carrot was jealous of me dating Allen. Knowing we had finally been intimate struck a nerve with her. She was dating my brother – What the heck was going on here??

After finishing with the kids, I went straight to Carrot and asked her what was up. "I saw him first." She said. I reminded her that she was not available and that she had introduced him to me. "I know, but you know how it is. I just thought maybe if Richard and I broke up, Allen would be right here. I know he likes me. If you were not here, we would be together." I gave her that look -- the look that says "are you kidding me?" Instead I asked if she were going to break up with Richard. "Of course not, I'm going to marry him. I'm pregnant – remember?" That answered everything. Carrot was having an attack of the "what if's." She was my friend and I knew she would never try to take Allen away from me.

In late July the summer was winding down. We all, Carrot, Richard, Allen and I, gathered together to go to the county fair. We walked around the exhibit and there was a person sitting at a drafting table designing a dress. At another table was a drawing of a beautifully appointed interior of a room. There was also a girl demonstrating the proper way to apply make-up. Carrot and I were intrigued. It was an exhibit booth of a school specializing in modeling, fashion design and interior design. They were having a drawing for a free scholarship. I slipped my entry blank into the slot and promptly forgot about it.

A few weeks later, my parents called to tell me that it was important that they speak with me. I wouldn't be able to be there until Saturday and that meant two days to rack my brains trying to think about what I did wrong.

What I did wrong was think that I had done something wrong. The school had called and told my parents that I had won a scholarship. I had been making my own clothes since I was in ninth grade. They both saw this as an opportunity for me to learn fashion design skills. The fact that they also taught things about social graces really appealed to my mother. For my mother, it was a finishing school. For my father, it was an acceptable trade. For me it was moving on in my life.

Wow! I had a plan! I was excited. I would be living in an apartment with some other students in the city. I would be on my own, but still going to school. I would need a part-time job, but I was no stranger to work. This was exactly what I needed. I would be a "finished" fashion designer.

Allen was excited for me. The summer was ending and he needed to get back to school and work. There would be no "next" school break. He would continue to visit his father on holidays, but I would be either working or visiting my own family. We were sure we would connect at various points in time in the future, but we knew, for the most part, our relationship was probably over.

I didn't know that enrolling in that particular school and moving to that particular apartment complex, would be one of those life-changing experience.

JUST LIKE MY FATHER

I've heard that all little girls want to grow up and marry men just like their Daddy. That seems logical. The person of the opposite sex who is the most protective of you would make the best life partner. For good or ill, it does happen to most young ladies.

For most children there is a time of rebellion in the teen years. If the child is a "late bloomer" the rebellion can spill over into the late teens and early twenties. It is a time when every aspect of their current life is directly opposed to what they think they want in their future life. That's what happened to me.

MY NAME IS RILEY

I only know what Riley has told me about his childhood and what I have learned has come from years of prodding. While the Logan family was open and demonstrative, Riley's family seemed extremely private with very few displays of affection. I asked Riley once if his parents told him he loved him. He said love in his childhood home was implied and assumed. His father never actually said the words and his mother seldom displayed expressions of love. An accomplishment was more likely to be met with a handshake and a pat on the back rather than a hug and kiss.

Fredrick James Riley was born late in the summer of 1939. His parents had waited to have children until they were in their late 30s. They were delighted to finally be starting a family. Before Fredrick was a year old, Mrs. Riley was expecting the second of her two sons, William.

They were a typical family living in the breadbasket of the country. Mr. Riley was a salesman and Mrs. Riley was a secretary for a prominent local surgeon. Their house was meticulously kept clean of any clutter. There was not one speck of untidiness anywhere. Even the accumulated dirty dishes were kept out of sight by placing them under the sink until there was time to wash them. Cleanliness was a high priority in this house.

There was a schedule to be kept in the Riley house which meant there was a time for everything and everything was allotted a specified amount of time. Riley had two hours to complete his homework. He sat at his father's big desk being careful not to disarrange any of the items that had a home on the desktop. When he was done everything was put back into the exact order it was prior to the homework session.

Fredrick took a bold step by telling his parents that he hated his name and preferred just to be called Riley. His parents did not comply with the request, but his schoolmates happily obliged.

The two children were very close as young boys, but as they grew into their teen years they discovered their interests were in opposing directions. Riley was an easy child – he had enjoyed school and never broke his parent's rules. William was artistic and seemed to march to the tune of his own drummer. By the time they reached high school, they were no longer each other's constant companions – they ran in different circles.

Riley was a scholar and excelled at everything he attempted. He was a band member, good looking and very popular. He graduated at the top of his class with honors. He was destined to do great things and his school mates voted him as the most likely to succeed.

Riley entered a local four-year college where he continued to do well scholastically. He became engaged to a beautiful girl and his mother was extremely pleased at the prospective union. The future was bright and everyone was excited for his future.

At the end of his second year, Riley became restless. The usual challenge of scholastics was no longer keeping his attention. He started becoming interested in the young co-eds on campus and it was difficult for him to remain faithful to his fiancé. He broke off the engagement and, much to his mother's disappointment, decided not to return for his third year. Instead, Riley walked into the Army recruiter's office to sign up. But the recruiter had gone to lunch, so he left and went next door where he found the Navy recruiter to be more than happy to have him sign on the dotted line. Riley was going to see the world while riding the waves of the ocean. He was excited to start this new adventure.

Mr. and Mrs. Riley were devastated. This was not what they had planned for their golden child. He was supposed to become a nuclear physicist or scientist or some other professional that reeked of intelligence. He was not supposed to be gallivanting around the world with a bunch of drunken sailors. If he were determined to have a military life, the least they expected of him was to go in as an officer rather than a low-life seaman.

After only two years of Navy life, Riley, who looked dapper in his white uniform, met the woman who would become his first wife. Laura was beautiful and stood an inch above Riley's 5'8" frame. They were a striking couple. She was shy and innocent and he was bright and handsome. They become astute members of a mutually agreed upon church and were married within a year of meeting.

They were a normal couple and lived a normal military life. A family was started with the birth of their first boy, James. They transferred across country to the east coast and the sailor began a life at sea. But, Laura had never lived so far from her family and was feeling a bit abandoned by her sea-going husband. During one of the long deployments, she found comfort with a shore-based Marine. When Riley returned, he found her in the arms of another man. He was enraged and the two men had a short, but violent encounter.

Riley and Laura wanted to stay together and began trying to work out their issues. She became pregnant once again. Riley thought things were getting back to normal when he was forced to leave for another deployment. This time, when he returned, the family was gone. Laura had taken their little boy and gone back to California before he returned from sea. She was living with her family when she gave birth to their second boy, Grant.

Riley visited Laura as often as he could until he began to dislike all the travelling. The couple tried to make it work, but Riley was angry, distrustful and resentful. He developed an attitude of expecting to be hurt. It was a matter of "do unto women first before they do unto you." The prospects of saving his marriage became dimmer by the day.

In Riley's opinion, his Navy career was also to blame for destruction of his marriage. He was beginning to long for a job without such high demands on his personal time and lifestyle. He had been in the Navy for seven years and was growing tired of moving and restricted attire and chains of command. When his tour of duty was complete, he did not re-enlist. Instead he headed to California where he would either work out his marital problems or enjoy being a bachelor in the highly social city by the bay – San Francisco.

Riley had enough money to last 30 days. After that, he would be unemployed and homeless. He took up residence at the Oakland YMCA and had no trouble finding a job as a technical writer for an electronics firm in Berkeley. He took his first paycheck and moved into an upscale apartment building with two roommates.

He visited his wife every other weekend, but was always anxious to get back to the hustle of the city. His efforts to make his marriage work seemed to be getting pushed farther and farther down his priority list. He didn't want a confrontation with Laura. He didn't want to lose the possibility of having his family if he should find that his desire for bachelorhood was just a fleeting fancy. He wanted to keep them on the back burner. He decreased his visits to once a month and then every six weeks.

There were lots of women who were willing to keep Riley company. He had a gift of being able to draw them in and then letting them go. His roommates were in awe as he would keep several women interested at the same time. He reveled in his "playboy-ness". No complications. No commitments. No messy emotional attachments. His life was exactly as he wanted it to be. He had no idea that apple strudel cookies would make such a huge change in his life. Things would never be the same.

AND THEN THERE WAS YOU

I started going to the fashion design/modeling school in the first week of September. I had found a part-time job at JC Penney's and settled in with my two roommates, Gina and Marie. It was fun getting to know these two girls. I had no history with them and I found myself being open to trusting them. In time, I would learn that they never once abused my trust. Other than Carrot, I had never before had this kind of friendship. Maybe because I was more mature, I welcomed them with an open heart.

Gina was short, small, reddish blonde hair and bright green eyes which suited her casual friendly personality. In contrast Marie was tall, thin, dark brown hair, hazel eyes. She was stately and proper. Her laughter was barely noticeable – quiet and not freely expressed.

We lived in an upscale apartment building which had amenities such as an indoor swimming pool, a gym and underground parking. I felt as though I was living in the lap of luxury.

We each had our own reasons for attending this school. Marie wanted to a model, while Gina was more interested in interior design. The combination worked.

Acutely aware that we were all, in fact, attending a "modeling" school, we were careful about our appearance. We ate healthy, drink hot water and lemon toddies every morning, used the gym and walked everywhere. Well… we had to walk because none of us had a car. We were very close to being right "downtown" so walking anywhere was an easy thing to do.

In keeping with eating right… we had only vanilla wafer cookies in the apartment. No Oreos, Sugar Wafers, Chocolate Chip… just plain old Vanilla Wafers. We could live without all that sugar, but we had to have SOMETHING other than celery for snacking.

We were basking in the sun that was baking the concrete of our apartment balcony. We were on the third floor on the courtyard side. The box of vanilla wafers was being passed around as we lied to each other about how delicious they were. It was a good afternoon.

In the courtyard there was a man lying out soaking up the rays. He had next to him a bag of Apple Strudel cookies and just the sight of that bag sent goose bumps up our spine. The cookies were more attractive than the man. Who cared about the man – there were Apple Strudel cookies for goodness sake. We were three young ladies jones-ing for sugar and there it was just two floors down… it was calling to us.

One of us would have to make a move. We were deep into a discussion as to which one of us would make a play for the guy in order to get the cookies. He looked kinda cute from this distance. He didn't look like a geezer or a pervert. Sometime during this discussion the box of wafers slipped off the balcony and landed right on the guys head. The other two girls scrambled for the door and left me out there – standing on the balcony – with him looking right up at me. I was a deer in the headlights.

"Do you want your cookies back?" he asked.

"I'll trade you mine for yours. How about that?" I called down to him.

"OK. Meet me at the second floor lobby." He answered.   Yea!!! Mission accomplished!! I'd just meet him, make the trade and we'd be done with the whole thing. I swear the other two girls were salivating as I left the apartment.

I went to the second floor and he was already there. He handed me the bag of cookies. I couldn't just take them and run back upstairs, so I made small talk. The small talk turned into us sitting on the sofa and talking some more. I don't know how long we were talking, but Marie showed up and said she was wondering where I was. Right after her was Gina. We were all sitting around in the lobby talking and eating cookies.

I thought to myself that when we left the lobby that would be the end of this guy named Riley. We would go our separate ways and that would be it. What kind of name was Riley anyway?? He must be a hundred years old – but he didn't look like it.

We learned that he was 26 years old and had just had a birthday. He shared an apartment with two other men on the second floor. He was a technical writer for an electronics manufacturer. His voice and laughter were soft. His brown wavy hair was neatly cut and in place. His big brown eyes reminded me of a lost puppy dog. He grew up in Iowa and came to California on a Navy transfer and never wanted to leave. We learned a lot in the space of about an hour.

Getting up to leave, Gina turned and said… "Why don't you come to dinner at our place this evening?" I looked at her and wondered – could she be interested in this guy? Sure he was handsome and all… but none of us had ever expressed any interest in getting involved with any man while we were focusing on school. He eagerly accepted and we went our separate ways.

Gina and Marie did all the cooking for our very first real dinner guest. Just the idea of having company was exciting. The fact that this was "male" company made it ever better. Steak, Baked Potatoes, Green Salad and Apple Pie… that was the menu. We thought it best to stick to basics. We had to scrape the bottom of our wallets to buy the steak – but it all came together.

Sitting around our dinner table – which was all properly set according to all those etiquette books I had read as a child – the conversation was mostly about how we all got to where we were today.

I learned a lot about Riley in that conversation. He worked at a desk job in an office and didn't know much about cars let alone heavy equipment. He worked from 8-4 Monday through Friday and was off every weekend and holiday. He was a technical writer which in my mind meant he was able to write a sentence without any dangling participles and didn't end his sentences with a preposition.

But, I didn't really think I was very interested in him -- too much baggage. He was divorced with two little boys. I couldn't see myself as wanting to have anything to do with that situation. He was also nine years older than me – that's too much. My parents would never approve of him which would make my life difficult.

Gina, on the other hand, seemed very interested. And it seemed the feeling was mutual. But, when dinner was over and the table was cleared, Riley turned to me and asked if I would like to go for a walk. I didn't answer right away. I took my time because I wasn't about to steal a man of interest from my new roommate. Once I had managed to confirm that Gina was not in the least interested in Riley, I accepted the invitation.

The weather was perfect for an evening walk. It was cool but not cold and the stars lit up the sky with a silvery glow. Our apartment was only a block from the lake which had a walking path completely around it. Walking around the lake was a popular activity in this city.

We took a couple of detours which allowed us to walk by stores that had closed for the evening. The windows were lit and displayed their products vividly. We discussed the fashion and I was full of myself as I explained the history of the style of clothing. I was in my element.

At the very far end of the lake there is a pergola that juts right into the lake. Standing there you feel surrounded by the water and trees. It is truly a beautiful place. That evening the moon shone across the smooth water like a mirror. The stars got brighter as each hour took us deeper into the night.

That's where it happened. Riley kissed me. It was a sweet gentle kiss, but it was filled with passion. I forgot about the divorce, kids, age difference, I forgot all those red flags and enjoyed every second of that kiss.

We walked home, holding hands and talking about things that didn't really matter. I was surprised when he asked me to have dinner with him on Saturday evening. I wanted to say NO! Every fiber of my being screamed out STOP! He's too old!! He's divorced with kids!! But, it seemed I was outside myself listening as I heard the words flowing from my mouth... "I would love to have dinner with you." So much for being cautious.

I know that from the time of his invitation to the night of our dinner had to have at least 200 days. It could not have been only four days to Saturday. But it was a good thing I had those four days because I needed to prepare.

Gina and I wore the same size and we pulled pieces from both our wardrobes to make the perfect dinner-date outfit. Marie did my make-up and both girls helped with my hair by pulling my long blonde locks up into a sophisticated French roll. I looked a good two years older than my actual age – which I didn't want to divulge to Riley yet. I was pleased with the image that stared back at me in the full-length mirror.

Riley didn't have a car, but borrowed his roommates and we drove down to the wharf. Then we took an elevator up to the fourth floor of an old building. The doors opened and there was tropical décor everywhere you looked. There was a lobster tank with live creatures longing for an escape. Star fish were stuck in nets hanging from the ceiling and walls. The windows looked out over the docks that housed yachts and sailboats. The scene was something you would have found on a postcard from a Caribbean vacation.

It wasn't as though I had never been to a seafood restaurant before because I certainly had. My aunt once took me to a very exclusive one while visiting her in southern California. We sat in a grass hut type booth. There were rainfalls and hula dancers. That restaurant far surpassed the one on this date with Riley.

Looking over the menu, Riley suggested an appetizer – actually he told me what his appetizer would be and asked what I would like. I had never ordered appetizers before – it always just seemed like an expensive way to fill up before you got your real food. I was taught to save my appetite for the meat of the meal.

Salads – well shouldn't that just come with dinner? I had never heard of anyone ever ordering a special salad. And I had never seen one prepared at my tableside. Riley ordered the Caesar Salad for two and there they were. The result was delicious and I feel in love with those anchovy and raw egg concoctions. From that day forward my favorite salad has always been Caesar.

I was worried that I wasn't going to have room for the "real" part of dinner. I had ordered broiled scallops and I wouldn't want to appear as though I wasn't happy with the dish. But, to my surprise, my scallops arrived and I ate every single bite.

"Dessert?" Riley asked. Oh, I didn't think I could eat any dessert. But, he insisted we share a piece of cheese cake. I accepted and managed to get that down as well.

Finally finished with the food, we walked around the docks while admiring the boats. Then we took a drive in the borrowed red T-bird convertible. I put a scarf over my coif so we could put the top down. I felt like Grace Kelly with her Cary Grant. We drove outside the city and into the hills where we could have a good view of the city lights over the Bay as they outlined the Golden Gate Bridge.

Of course the view was only of interest for a short period. We moved on to kissing and "making out" like a couple of teenagers on Lover's Lane. There was no pressure for sex – just the two of us kissing. He made no bold advances and after about a half hour, we were on our way back home.

Although I was totally smitten with Riley, he was not my main priority in my life. I had school and work, and my long term career goals didn't really have a place for a husband. In my mind, if we moved beyond dating, I might have to give up my dreams to be what he wanted me to be rather than what I wanted to be. I was cautious. But Riley was persistent in wanting to advance to a sexual relationship. He wrote me "love notes" and left them on my door on his way to work. He met each night in the lobby of our building and kissed as the elevator went from the fourth floor to the garage. He told me he loved me and only wanted me to be successful at attaining my dreams. In a few months I was hooked. It still amazes me that he stayed around that long. I told myself, if he didn't love me, he would have walked away weeks ago.

I was hooked. I saw this man as being everything my father was not and I thought it was what I wanted. I thought he was my "dream come true." He was sophisticated, educated, etiquette-savy, white-collar, was supportive in my career goals, and he loved me… what more could a girl want?

Linda Bartee Doyne (aka Linda Jane Riley)

PART THREE

RED FLAGS AND YELLOW LIGHTS

We met in early July. In mid-October, Riley moved into his own studio apartment without roommates. In the last week of October, he lost his job. To this day, I am not sure of the circumstances around that job loss. He had been there for a couple of years and he seemed to be happy – but now he was collecting unemployment. I was too young to understand that this was a red flag.

I was working close to 40 hours a week at my job as a retail clerk and going to school full time. I spent my weekends with Riley.

Now that his income was greatly reduced, we didn't go out to fancy dinners anymore. It was more likely that a night out would mean going to Doggie Diner. Don't get me wrong – I loved Doggie Diner. But, I missed experiencing the different cuisines that Riley had made available. I missed going to Broadway plays and symphonies. But I was in love. Those things are small when love abounds. I wasn't in love with him for the dinners and plays. In my mind, I told myself to love him just for those "things" would make me shallow – and shallow was not what I wanted to be. He was still the same person without all the trappings – and the *person* was what my values told me was important.

I was in love because he was the man of my dreams even if he didn't fit the true definition anymore. If love is true, I believed I must "stand by my man." And so I stood firm when I should have run for the hills. I guess that's why I ignored all those warning signs flashing in my face like those flashing yellow lights atop a sawhorse in the middle of a construction zone.

In late November, I got pregnant. It was just before my 18th birthday. Riley refused to believe I was actually pregnant and refused to discuss it in any manner. I told Carrot and then my roommates, Gina and Marie. I didn't tell anyone else – certainly I did not and could not tell my parents. At least, I couldn't tell them until Riley accepted the fact that we were going to have a baby.

I was still working and had extra hours over the Christmas holidays. It seemed every time I got a great paycheck, Riley needed something for which he didn't have enough money. In order for him to go on job interviews, I paid for his $20 haircuts (I had never seen a man go do a hairdresser before – they always went to the barber shop and haircuts cost $2.50). I paid for car rentals and lunches and sometimes even dinners.

I remember one evening when we were in Riley's apartment. He had been to a doctor that day – I don't remember why. When we were sitting down to dinner, he told me that the doctor had told him he needed to stop drinking. At that point, I had never seen him drunk so I didn't really understand why the doctor would say this. In reality… maybe I had never seen him sober. I just acknowledged his statement and we went on with our evening.

In February, Riley was arrested for not paying his child support. I didn't know he wasn't paying it. In fact, I had no idea how much it was or any other facts about his obligations to his boys. I knew he had visited them regularly because on many occasions, I paid for the weekend long trips.

I never knew anyone who had ever even been to jail. Sure, I had friends who went to Juvenile Hall, but not to jail. The issue was resolved and he was back at home in just a couple of days. One more red flag.

In April, Riley finally got employment. He would be working for an electronics firm about 45 minutes from where we lived. The pay was acceptable and Riley seemed truly excited about his upcoming professional challenge. The location was actually good in my eyes because it was exactly half-way between where we lived now and where my family lived. I was very familiar with this smaller town and my imagination was running wild with thoughts of marriage and settling down closer to my family.

My flat tummy was starting to get a bump. I looked like maybe I had a few too many beers in my diet. Riley continued to tell me he wasn't sure I was pregnant. We still had not discussed it except in passing. Fed up with the situation, I went to an OB-GYN and got him to write a note that stated the facts of my pregnancy. I was due in August. It was final. Riley finally conceded to the overwhelming fact that a baby was on the way.

The same day I presented Riley with the note confirming my pregnancy, I learned that Riley was not REALLY divorced. In California during that time frame, the state had a mandatory one-year interlocutory. Riley's divorce wouldn't be final until the following November because his wife had not signed the papers until then.

What!!!! Are you kidding me!!! I think that was the first fight we had ever had. Had I known Riley was really married – there would never have been the first dinner with my roommates – no walk around the lake – no first kiss and absolutely NO seafood restaurants at the wharf!!

November – that was when I was paying for his visits to see his boys. Two weekends a month, what else came out of my pocket? Was he having conjugal visits with his wife – the wife that I thought wasn't?

It was only a few weeks later that I received my first phone call from Riley's wife, Karen. There would be several calls after this one. She accused me of having an affair with her husband. She told me that they were only separated because there was more work for Riley in the city rather than the small town where she lived with their boys. She informed me there would be no divorce.

Riley assured me that he would make this right. He professed his true love for me and said he would find a way to get the divorce with or without her consent. He said we would be married, but it would be after the baby was born. So what if it was a little late? We would still be married.

I had to tell my family about the pregnancy and insisted that we rent a car to make the trip to my parent's house. As a couple, we had been there before and things went pretty well. But, I was Daddy's girl... this was not going to go like the other visits. I called my mother and let her know we were coming so that I could insure my father's presence.

The driveway to my parent's house was lined with cars when we arrived. It looked like the gang was all here. I didn't like that because I only wanted to tell my parents. They should be the first to know and I didn't want a lot of family drama. I had already been through the fight with Riley and I didn't think I needed another one with my brothers.

My attempted expose turned into a family reunion and no mention was made of the fact that I was wearing a dress that could easy be construed as maternity clothing. Carrot took me aside and asked if I had told Mom and Daddy – I told her I couldn't with all the others around. I said I couldn't believe they couldn't tell from looking at me. She told me I was the skinniest five-month pregnant woman she had ever seen. No one would suspect.

A downturn in sales resulted in some layoffs at my job and I found myself unemployed. I was perfectly OK with that. Being pregnant and both working and going to school was exhausting. My roommates wanted to move to a different building that had rents well over my comfort zone. So they moved on and I moved into a studio apartment that I could afford on my own which was miles from the school, my ex-roomies and Riley's apartment.

Riley had moved into a place with his brother. He never mentioned having me move in and I wondered how things were going to work once his divorce was final and we were married. He told me he wanted this opportunity to be with his brother and how important it was for him to strengthen this bond. It was OK. My parents were still in the dark about the baby, so moving in with him would just cause more eyebrows to rise.

After a couple of attempts at making the trip to tell my parents about our news – we gave up. I love my family and they are all happy to see me when I come home – but I just couldn't manipulate having an audience with my parents alone. I was unbelievably frustrated at the whole situation. Each day that passed was more fuel on a fire that was just waiting for a striking match.

At some point, I felt a real need for support from someone, so I called my good friend, Allen. We had exchanged phone calls many times over the year, but had not seen each other. He was now enamored with a young woman, but the relationship was rocky. Both of us had egos that needed to be bolstered.

Allen arrived at my studio and we had the dinner I had prepared. We spent the rest of the evening talking about our love interests. We spooned on the sofa while lamenting each others situation. We came to a conclusion. We decided that neither of us had the relationship we wanted, but both of us loved the people who held our hearts. In spite of it all, we needed to make the most of what we had. It is what it is. Either we accepted it or we had to get out. Both of us agreed, we would rather accept it than to lose it. We were hopeless.

We ended the evening with Allen taking me to Riley's apartment. We knew we would always be friends and would always give each other support. We were there for each other.

One night in late June, Riley came to my studio and after a lovely dinner, he broached a subject that I had never even considered. He wanted me to NOT tell my parents I was pregnant. He suggested I could have the baby and they would never know. My response was something like -- it will become very obvious at Christmas when I show up with a bouncing bundle of joy. No – he insisted – you can give the baby up for adoption and no one would ever know.

I was so angry I was literally seeing red. How could he?? I stood up, marched to the telephone and dialed my parent's number. My mother picked up. I asked if she and Daddy were both there and could they both listen at the same time. Of course, they could. I looked straight at Riley and said, "I'm pregnant. My baby is due in August. I don't want to get married and I'm not sure what to do." Riley looked at me as though I had just killed his cat. "OK. We'll figure this out." That was my parent's response.

After the phone call, Riley came over to me. Tears were streaming down my face. He wrapped his arms around me and said – "I guess we're having a baby." At that moment – at the very moment – I did not have the courage to do what I should have done long ago – kicked him to the curb.

The phone call happened at 8 p.m.-ish. By 8 a.m.-ish everything I owned was packed into my cousin's truck and I was moved back to my family's home – almost two hours from Riley, Gina and Marie. I was 18 and therefore should have been able to make my own decisions. But, I was numb, lost, confused and needed the softness of my old bedroom to regroup.

I took a leave of absence from school. I just wanted to hibernate. Carrot visited me with her brand new handsome baby boy. But, I was inconsolable. I went into a deep depression and wanted nothing more than to spend my days sleeping in my room. I had lost the love of my life and the father of my child. I knew there would be no wedding, no happily ever after. Surrounded by people who loved me unconditionally, I was alone.

Thank goodness for my mother. She was a firm believer that a day that was not productive was just a wasted day. "You'll never have this day to live again – so make use of it while you can." She got me up, assigned me tasks, let me cook, and made me plan for how I was going to survive as a single parent. My parents offered to adopt my baby and raise it as their own. But, I couldn't see doing that.

My father was angry. As he put it – he never expected this from me. Of all the kids he thought I was the one with the best head on my shoulders. Disappointing or angering my father was never anything I ever wanted to do. I always wanted, needed his approval. Now I was just another one of those women without values. Losing his respect was almost as bad as ending my relationship with Riley.

Back in the day, when a girl got pregnant the boy was obligated to marry her. It was the RIGHT thing to do. Once the baby was born the hope was that the couple would have bonded over the birth enough to make the marriage work. Sometimes it happened and sometimes it didn't. It was a crap shoot. But, my father wanted this man to make an honest woman of me and so he demanded that Riley come to our house for a "sit down."

Riley was charming. My father was diplomatic. My mother was pissed. I was ready to run for cover. My father offered to pay Riley to get a Mexican divorce so that we could marry and give the baby a name. Riley agreed. But I knew he was just telling my father what he wanted to hear. I knew there would be no quicky divorce and/or shotgun wedding. After Riley was gone, I took my father aside and told him not to hold his breath. That Riley was lying to him and I was on my own.

Then the phone calls started. Riley called nearly every day. And if I didn't want to talk to him, my mother would force the phone into my hand and make me talk to him. He drove out to see me and was genuinely concerned for me. He wanted to repair our relationship.

I was stagnant at my parent's house. Out in the country where we were, there was no public transportation. There were lots of things within walking distance, but I was so pregnant and the heat was so stifling, walking anywhere would not have been a good idea. I literally had nothing to do.

My aunt who was a single mom, offered to let me come stay with her. She lived only a few blocks from my old studio apartment – so I would be back in the city. I could help her take care of her little boy while she worked in her beauty salon. It was the perfect situation. My parents agreed. I moved right in.

My little cousin was the extreme of spoiledness, but he was adorable. I loved him very much, in spite of all the frustration he produced. He was just a little guy – about four years old. But he was four trying to go on forty.

I missed my mother very much. I needed her. I called her almost daily and didn't care how much money each call cost. No one could take her place. Even though, our relationship was often strained… I needed my Mommy.

A month later, Brian Riley arrived. My mother and Riley were there. That is, after my mother found Riley, he came to the hospital. She had to leave several messages with his brother – who was evasive as to where Riley was. Because Riley had wanted to re-build our relationship, Mom was a bit surprised that he was not waiting by the phone just in case today was the today. Where was he?

When Riley came into my room, I remember him saying "We had a baby. Ain't that neat." I asked if he had seen him and he said answered affirmatively. He told me Brian was perfect and that he had to go. I was in the hospital three days which was a normal maternity stay during those days. Although he called everyday, Riley never returned to visit me in the hospital. My mother was there every single day.

While I was in the hospital, my aunt received her phone bill. She told my parents, I could not return to her home when I was released from the hospital. She could not afford to have me live with her, since I didn't seem to want to obey the rule of "no long-distance phone calls." She also was dismayed at the fact that it appeared as though I was forgiving Riley and would end up back together with him. I was hurt, but like a good, little girl, I went back to my parents' home with my babe in arms.

I was there for about a month. I was getting stronger and needed to move on with my life. I couldn't see Riley while I was there and the distance was really becoming an issue. I asked Gina and Marie if I could stay with them temporarily and they were more than happy to have me back. Brian, being the only baby around, got lots of attention from everyone in the complex. It was the perfect set up but I needed my own space.

I found a small apartment on the edge of an iffy part of town. It was cheap, but the rent combined with the money I spent on bug spray, I could have been living in a penthouse in a high-rise. It was OK.

The other tenants were good neighbors who doted on Brian and were always willing baby-sitters.

I got a job for an insurance company in San Francisco. It was decent money, but by the time I paid the sitter, there wasn't much left. After 6 months, I decided that Riley and I needed to have a long talk.

It was during this time that I met the reason why Riley could not be found when I was in labor. Her name was Sandy. She was married. And she knew all about me. I finally realized that Riley was not serious about marrying me or making us a family. I had only been convenient. He finally confessed that he had kept me hanging on because he did not want to risk the ire of my father and being arrested for statutory rape since I was only 17 when I got pregnant.

It was finally clear to me. All the red flags waving with hurricane force and all the yellow blinking lights – I could see them all clearly now. It was like I had walked out of a fog. And I decided that my baby and I needed a better life and I set out to get just that.

I left Riley behind, met someone else and a year later, I got married. It didn't last long. Only a little over two years and just long enough for me to get pregnant and have my daughter, Alea. We ended the marriage when Alea was only three months old. But I was a strong, confident woman and was able to take care of my little family without the aid of a man.

The following Christmas, I was doing some shopping in a little village-like area of Oakland, CA, when I literally walked right into Riley. We had a drink, which turned into dinner. He had re-enlisted in the Navy and was home visiting his brother for the holidays. He was verifiably divorced. By the time the evening was over, I had promised him a dinner date for the next evening. I also promised he could visit his son and meet my eight-month old baby girl.

Riley returned to his duty station in Norfolk, VA, but was back at my house within a few months. He had 30 days leave and he used it all re-building his relationship with me, Brian and was falling in love with Alea. By the time he was ready to return to duty, we agreed I would move to Norfolk and we would build our life together. Just the way it should have been before all the chaos.

A NAVY LIFE WITH RILEY

Gina, my ex-roommate, married a sailor and was living in Norfolk. When I arrived with my kids in tow, she and her husband met me at the airport. I spent a few days with them while waiting for Riley to return from sea. Gina and I had not seen each other for several years, but we re-connected as through no time had ever passed.

We talked for hours into the night about everything in our lives. And just before we finished our conversation and went off to our respective beds, she asked a question... "Do you really want to get back on the Riley Roller Coaster from Hell?" She could have asked if I thought he had changed or if I thought it would work this time. But she didn't and I could only answer with... "I love him."

NARROW STREETS

Riley picked me up from Gina's and took his young family to our new home. It was a small community of families who resembled our own. Young military couples with a child or two made up the majority of the neighborhood demographic.

Our house was a townhome that once served as officer's family quarters during WWII. There were four townhomes in the building essentially creating a four-plex. The walls were solid and the construction was sturdy. We each had our own fenced in yard that backed up to an alley.

The tree-lined streets were so narrow that only one car could fit as it travelled down the road. A car in one direction was always pulling over so another could pass by in the opposite direction.

We didn't have a car. We were within walking distance to the business circle where there was a grocery and drug store. There was also a soda shop, hardware store and post office. Riley commuted with a shipmate to the nearby naval base where he was home ported. Everything we needed was right there.

Although Riley may have been vertically challenged, he was strong and brilliant. He was set in his ways and routine. Getting him to be spontaneous was impossible. If he switched coffee brands – well that was spontaneous enough for him. He was a planner who preferred orderly repetition.

Each evening when he arrived home after work he removed his jacket, took off his shoes, put on his slippers and then he would wait. He would stand in the hallway and wait. I would come out of the kitchen and give him a kiss, ask about his day. He responded, but he didn't leave the entryway. He was waiting.

Brian would get up and come over to his father and give him a hug while being a little irritated because it meant he would have to stop whatever was holding his attention at the time. But, Alea... well...

she would bounce through the room and almost literally climb her father's frame to get into his arms. Once there, her little arms would wrap around his neck. Then, as though it were choreographed, she would trill his handlebar moustache between her tiny fingers. The wait was over. Riley could now head upstairs to get out of his sailor suit and into his real clothes.

There wasn't a lot of bad weather, but when it hit us – it hit us hard. This particular holiday season we were dodging snowflakes on an almost daily basis. Walking to the grocery store was nearly impossible. And, it was almost Christmas and Santa had not done much shopping. We were spending quite a bit on taxi cabs to run our necessary errands. So, Santa's budget was dwindling.

We were down to our last $50 when we finally made it to the drug store on Christmas Eve. They didn't have a lot, but we spent the entire $50 on cheap plastic toys that parents now-a-days would ban from their homes -- A plastic dump truck, a few little cars, some pop-beads, a little doll, some coloring books and crayons, socks and two hats. We still had some left for candy, a couple of oranges and apples for the stockings. We're talking about nearly 40 years ago – so what would be consider now as just a little bit of money went a long way.

On our way home, we passed the Christmas tree lot. The lot was closing down and to keep from having to burn the left over trees, they were giving them away. We dragged one home along with our other goodies. It was still early and Brian and Alea were delighted with the short bushy tree. It was given a place of honor in the corner next to the big boxy black and white TV.

We drank hot chocolate, ate caramel apples, cookies and carrot sticks. We strung popcorn and made paper chains and hung them on the tree. Then we decided to put out a snack for Santa. Riley insisted that Santa was trying to trim a few pounds so we set out carrot and celery sticks instead of cookies.

Once the kids were tucked into bed, I started to work on wrapping the gifts. I wanted to have a large "Santa" toy unwrapped under the tree, but we didn't have one. So I meticulously wrapped each gift and placed it under the tree in a way that made it look like there was a lot more than there was.

We were up early on Christmas morning. We were preparing our coffee when we realized we were out of milk. We absolutely could not be out of milk. Alea would surely have a terrible temper tantrum if she did not have her milk with breakfast. We thought maybe we could say it was a holiday so everyone would drink apple juice, but we knew that really wasn't going to fly.

So... in the middle of a snow storm... on what had to be the coldest day in the history of the world... Riley bundled up his body and walked the three blocks to the store. I watched him disappear into the swirls of little white clouds.

Just as he was returning both the kids were making their way down the stairs. He looked awful – cold and frozen. Bits of the hair that had been exposed looked frosty. Riley stood in the entryway, removed his jacket and he waited. Brian passed Riley by with a "Hi Dad" and as he turned the corner, he yelled "Whoaaaa!" when he saw the gifts under the tree. Alea, climbed up to her father's face and started to twirl his moustache. Instead of a giggle, I heard her scream.

The scream turned into a little whimpering cry as she looked down and saw she had broken the frozen handlebar off Daddy's face!! She looked at Riley with tears in her eyes and she looked at me as though I should try to glue it back on. Riley told her, "It's OK. Daddy can grow another one. You can help me cut the other side off. Let's go see what Santa has brought." My love for Riley swelled at that moment. I could love no man more than I loved him. He was my life, my love and the father of my children.

The gifts were opened and there were smiles all around. It didn't seem to matter that they didn't cost very much. Brian drove his truck from one end of the house to the other. He loaded the cars into the back of the truck and unloaded them at some imagined dumping ground. Alea immediately undressed her doll and re-dressed her. They both colored and played. Riley sat in his overstuffed chair and worked in his crossword puzzle book, looking up occasionally to check on the kids. I cooked Christmas dinner and enjoyed my sense of secure happiness.

Riley left his moustache just the way it was for the entire day. Then, just before bed, he and Alea went to the bathroom armed with a small pair of scissors and they ceremoniously trimmed the other side of his hairy lip.

SECURITY RISK

Because Riley was on a fast-attack submarine, he held a top secret security clearance. I really didn't think it had anything to do with me. It was his deal, his job, his status. I couldn't have been more wrong.

Riley was deployed overseas. For a submariner that means the sailor is out of contact. Literally. This was before cell phones, e-mail, tweeting, or Skype. Communication was maintained between spouses via the good old snail mail system. When the boat was out to sea, not moored at any port, there was no mail in or out. Letters from the wives were still mailed and a date was put on the outside of the envelope so the sailor knew in which order to open them. Men would receive mail in batches. The spouses would usually just get a letter a day for about ten days, and then… nothing for weeks on end. During those long dry spells, the same letters were read over and over again. Our letters ran the gauntlet of newsy, sweet and loving to down right x-rated. Sometimes we would even argue through the mail system. It was OK. Everyone was just happy to have something in the mail box.

I was working a part-time job in an office. I came home from work one day to find two well-dressed men sitting in my living room with the baby-sitter. I was happy I had just come from work because I was dressed professionally. If I had just been spending the day at home, I would have been in baggy jeans and a T-shirt. Being dressed in a dress and heals made me feel like I was more on equal ground.

They stood up as I entered the room. I stated that I was Linda and extended my hand as I asked if I could help them with something. They introduced themselves. I don't remember their names now, so I'll just call them Moe and Joe.

They told me they were following up on Riley's security status and needed to interview me as a part of the process. OK. I thought that made sense and I really had nothing to hide.

I was asked if I had ever been onboard the submarine. Of course, I had many times. I went there whenever Riley had to serve a 24 hour duty set. I would go for dinner and we would visit until sunset and then I would go home. I found the inside of the sub to be very confining and didn't like to stay for long. Whenever I was there, I focused on Riley and not the surroundings.

When the Moe and Joe asked what I had SEEN during my visits to the sub, I couldn't really give them specifics. To me, the whole inside looked like it was packed with grey and black boxes. There was a glass type table where the periscope was, but other than that; I wasn't sure what to tell them. So I told them the truth.

When I said black boxes – I thought Moe and Joe's eyes would pop out of their heads. They started asking me question after question about those boxes. Did Riley ever talk about them? Did he tell me what they were used for? What did I know about those boxes?

Come on… they were just boxes of all different sizes and shapes. Riley and I never discussed them except he did tell me they contained electronic stuff. I didn't really care what was in them. I have to admit I did enjoy looking through the periscope. The huge light table used for navigational mapping was something I could envision using in drafting sewing patterns. But what interested me most when I visited Riley onboard was what was on the galley's dinner menu. On Friday night's they served lobster and that was my favorite night to visit.

The men ended the interview and I thought the whole thing was over. WRONG! They were waiting on my doorstep a few days later after I had done some grocery shopping. They helped me bring in my bags and watched as I put away the food. In celebration of a co-worker's birthday, I was planning a special dinner. I had gotten some fresh crab legs for the occasion. They took special interest in those crabs. How could I afford crab on a petty officer's salary? I reminded them that I also brought money into the house. Who was the co-worker? What was our relationship? Could they see my bank statements? Why wasn't Riley and I married yet?

I was clearly getting irritated and told them if they wanted more information they would have to bring something tangible that gave them the right to inspect my personal life. I took the sleeve of each one and guided them to the door.

The baby-sitter and I both noticed a plain black car parked down and across our tiny street. Two men were sitting in the car and I could feel them watching my house. I didn't have any idea what they thought they would find. I was just a mom and wife going through my life as best as I could. I wasn't frightened, I was irritated. Let 'em watch me – I had nothing to hide.

One Sunday morning I woke up to icy rain. The black car was across the street. It looked cold and dark. I took out a serving tray and a coffee carafe. I added two mugs, some cream and sugar and some fresh baked coffee cake onto the tray. Then I put on my warmest clothing and took the tray out to the car.

The hot coffee sent steamy clouds and the smell of rich, warm goodness into the air. I tapped on the window and it was immediately rolled down. I told them, if they were insisting on sitting out in the rain, that I might as well try to warm them up. A little while later the car was gone and the tray was sitting on my porch. The coffee and cake were gone and there was a note – "Thank you." I never saw the car again.

I heard nothing from Moe or Joe for almost a month. We were halfway through the deployment and I was looking forward to having my man back within my reach. We were on the countdown.

The next time Moe and Joe arrived at my house, they had an official looking document that said I needed to hand over the letters Riley had written during the deployment. They assured they would be reviewed and returned promptly. I handed over the entire shoebox, as I mumbled that I hoped I didn't find out they were really just scam artists trying to get fodder for their next porn novels.

I made weekly phone calls to the numbers on the business cards they had left me. I always asked the same question – when would they be returning my letters? I didn't understand what the hold up could be. The letters were never about the Navy or the submarine. They were about us and our family and our plans. In one letter, written shortly after the boat's departure, I told Riley I thought I might be pregnant. Then two more letters later, I told him I was not going to have a baby after all. His letter to me was sweet and encouraging. How could that possibly be a threat to our country's security?

My weekly phone calls turned into two and three times a week and sometimes twice a day. I was not just irritated anymore, I was flat out angry.

But, the good thing about the experience was that I was finding my spunk. In the past, I had always just succumbed to people in authority, especially men. I seldom stood up for myself. Moe and Joe made me furious and I came out of my timid fear of men to firmly plant my feet and say – "No more!"

I marched myself in the office of Naval Investigative Services and asked who the officer was who supervised Moe and Joe. I was told that person was not available. So I asked for the commander. Again,

I was told he was not available. Next I asked for the director. I thought maybe I wasn't using the right words for "who is in charge here", so I kept trying. Each time I was told that person was not available. Finally, I said it's OK, I would wait. I settled in with my crocheting and made myself comfortable. When it got to be close to lunch time, I opened up my bag and pulled out my sandwich and chips. The sandwich was tuna with lots of onions – quite odiferous. I read my book, wrote a letter to Riley and just waited.

It took about four hours before they realized I wasn't going anywhere and I was shown to a well-appointed office. The uniformed man behind the desk asked me what he could do for me. I told him I wanted my letters back. It was simple. If I did NOT have the letters back within 48 hours, I would have my attorney be in touch with them.

By the time I got home, Moe and Joe were at my house – with my box of letters. I signed a receipt and they left.

I opened the box while feeling as though had been violated and reached in for one of my precious letters. I opened it and was shocked to see just about every other sentenced to have been blacked out with a Sharpie type marker. I immediately called the man behind the desk. He told me the blackened sentences were a threat and had been redacted. I had memorized those letters from reading them over and over again – I knew what had been "redacted." I saw no reason why telling Riley that I would like to take a weekend off to ourselves in Williamsburg, would be a threat to our security. I was dumbfounded. I was angry. I lost respect for the authority of NIS.

When Riley returned home, we hired a lawyer. Riley, the lawyer and I went to NIS and confronted them with the letter issue. The conversation was simple. If Riley was a threat, take away his clearance, but if they continued to harass me, the lawyer would force them to legally justify their actions.

I received a letter of apology and Riley not only retained his security status, he passed the chief's test and put on the chief's hat. We were transferred to Groton, CT which was the beginning of the end of my life as I knew it.

DO YOU LOVE ME?

Riley would be a member of the commissioning crew of a brand spanking new submarine. He was ecstatically happy for the new assignment. He had put a submarine in commission before and enjoyed being a part of the boat's birth. I was ecstatically happy because it would mean he would be home almost every night without runs at sea.

I didn't make the move to Connecticut with Riley. He would go on his last deployment with his current command and when he returned (six months later), he would go to Groton. He would get established at the new command and find us housing. By the time the kids and I arrived, Riley would have a place for us to settle into.

Riley left for deployment and I left for California to spend time with my family. Once Riley arrived in Connecticut, we talked every Sunday morning. It was our routine. I got up early and called the Chief's Quarters. It gave him time to eat breakfast and have a cup of coffee in hand for our talk. In those days it was expensive to make long-distance calls, so we limited ourselves to one a week. We would spent about a half-hour going over what the kids were doing, what my family was doing and what places he had looked at for our new home. It seemed to me everything was going fine. We were on schedule. I had even found a temporary job to give us some extra money and I was saving everything I could.

One Sunday Riley didn't answer the phone. He was not in the barracks and he had not left a message for me. I was confused and didn't understand what could have possibly kept him from our telephone date.

Riley ended up calling me from the apartment of a shipmate and his wife, Susan and Jim. He had gone there for a party on Friday and decided to stay the weekend. I thought that was good, he was making connections. In my mind these people would be my friends as well as his. The feeling of impending friendship was reinforced with each phone call when Riley would tell me that he was looking forward to introducing his family to their family. He always told me how much he missed me and how great it would be when we could be together again.

After that it seemed that Riley was always at Susan and Jim's home. Eventually, he moved in with them. I was still OK with all that. Maybe we could get an apartment in the same complex. I imagined neighbors who were already friends. I imagined the same bond of being a wife of a husband assigned to the same boat.

When I would talk to Riley he would tell me how great it was to live with this couple and their three kids. The kids behaved excellently and Riley had become a sort of uncle. So now... my kids would have built-in playmates. I'm still not seeing any of this as being a bad thing. And still, Riley continued with his declarations of love for his own family.

But the phone calls were coming less often now. It was not unusual for me to have to call several times before actually talking to Riley. When we did talk our conversations seemed to be shorter and shorter. I was anxious. I wanted our family to be together. The kids wanted their father. I wanted my family back.

I decided I had been separated from Riley long enough. I needed to take action. The young lady that had turned into an imitable force and impatiently waited in the NIS office was back. Not only was she back, she was determined to put an end to all this separation nonsense.

I called Riley and asked him if he was still wanted our family. I asked if he loved and/or missed me and the kids. I asked if he wanted me to come to Connecticut. I asked him if there were a way I could be there tomorrow, would he be happy? He answered in the affirmative to each point-blank question. I told him that was good because I would be arriving the next day at Hartford International Airport. I also told him that if he did not pick me up at the airport, I would be on the next flight back to California. This was a do or die situation. Either he acted or our relationship was dead.

HAND ME THAT LAMPSHADE

I peered out the window of the airplane, searching for any indication that Riley was waiting for me. But, I was on the wrong side of the plane and the only things visible were the lights of other landing planes. Hartford Airport wasn't very big and I would have to disembark and walk across the pavement to the waiting area. Both of the kids were sound asleep and making the trek to the terminal was going to take some finesse. I hung back and waited for everyone else to disembark. Then a flight attendant hoisted Alea into her arms as I grabbed up Brian and my bag.

I didn't see anyone familiar and was thinking that I was glad I had made reservations to return to California the next morning. I had a motel room waiting for me and if Riley didn't show, I was prepared. His presence at the airport would determine the rest of my life.

Then I saw him. He was waiting for us just beyond the gate. Alea was barely awake, but she knew her Daddy when she saw him and she ran into his arms. We loaded everything into the borrowed car and we headed for Groton. I sat close to Riley as though we were teenagers going out on a date. I was so happy we were together again and so happy I wouldn't need those other reservations that I had waiting.

"I really hope you can keep these kids in line. The Rittenhouse's children are extremely well behaved and I don't want Brian and Alea to embarrass me." It was a quiet statement. He didn't say he was happy we were there. He was concerned that we would not be a thorn in his side. I moved across the seat to the window and watched as the silhouetted trees passed by. "If you are so concerned about that and don't really want us here, you can take us back to the motel and we can be out of your life." I managed to reply. "Don't be silly," he said and he kept driving.

We stayed with the Rittenhouse family for a very uncomfortable two months until we managed to snag an apartment just below theirs' in the same complex. There were several other families in our complex that were a part of the crew. It was a close-knit group – we were each other's surrogate families. I longed for my real family and felt that I only barely fit in with this crowd.

I got a job at the local newspaper working nights as a paste-up artist and typographer. It was perfect. I loved the job and I didn't have to get a babysitter because Riley was home before I had to go to work. If he wasn't home, someone else in the complex always was.

Besides the newspaper job, I baby-sat for five other kids in the complex during the day. The extra money was a blessing and I loved the kids – it was a perfect fit.

We'd been there a while when I started to see a drinking pattern – not so much in Riley -- but in everyone around us.

Every Friday at least five shipmates and their spouses gathered in the common area outside our apartment. Everyone brought food to grill and booze to drink – and drink – and drink. People fell down drunk in the yard and on my floor. The party lasted until Sunday evening. This was our typical weekend for almost a year. I didn't like it, but I was told by several of the wives that I just needed to go with it and loosen up. I should be happy that Riley didn't get as drunk as all the other guys.

There were small intimate parties and large extravagant balls – all centered around getting drunk. It felt as though it were a contest to see who could get drunk the fastest and who could start throwing up first.

I watched it all go down like an alien from another planet. It seemed so absurd to me. These weren't fraternity brothers on a Saturday night. These were men assigned a task of helping to safeguard our country. Knowing this didn't make me feel so safe. I doubted their abilities to perform their duties and I doubted their superior's ability to recognize that the crew may not have the maturity to perform appropriately. On the other hand, most of the officers were younger than the enlisted crew members. Essentially and literally, they were all on the same boat – USS Drunken Immaturity.

But, I was the lucky one. My husband didn't get drunk every night. He took excellent care of our children and always had time to spend with me. I was happy – well -- there was this one little thing. But, it was probably just my imagination, so I ignored it – or I tried to ignore it.

One of the wives had told me that Riley had been dating one of the single women in the complex before I arrived. I thought the informant was just a troublemaker trying to drive a wedge between me and my husband.

I asked Susan about what I had heard and how silly I thought it was that the troublemaker was trying to create havoc. I was shocked to hear Susan telling me that Riley may have made an attempt at dating the woman, but that to her knowledge, it had never happened. Riley had once mentioned that I really wasn't much fun. Evidently, this other woman was a lot of FUN.

Riley and I had talked about the almost "other woman" and he had reassured me that there was never anything between the two of them. He told me he had just missed me so much and was very lonely.

At first, I walked away trying to figure out how I could me more FUN. But, I knew I was not fun. I worked two jobs and was often too tired (or just not interested) in joining in with the partiers. I seldom drank very much and was never the life of the party. I saw it as having two choices, join in or lose Riley.

I tried. I really, really tried. I went to every single party that took place when I was not working. I laughed and made jokes. I sipped on a drink or two. But, who was I kidding... I was not enjoying myself.

The party time was over for me. I let Riley go and do his thing. It didn't seem as though he was getting drunk as much as the others. While the younger crewmen were way over the legal limit, Riley and Jim seemed composed and unaffected by the alcohol.

I busied myself by cultivating other interests. I went back to school and took some writing and history classes. I became a den mother for Brian's Cub Scout pack. I volunteered for anything that the boats wives group was planning. I stopped caring about the parties and just focused on my family and myself.

FRIENDS SHARE EVERYTHING

We had moved to a townhouse and none of our neighbors were a part of the submarine's crew. We were in the end unit and only had one neighbor, Jane, a single woman with whom I became very good friends. It was good to have someone to talk to and shop with that had absolutely nothing to do with the Navy. She was at our house and over for dinner several nights a week. In a way, she became part of our family.

One day, Alea came running into the house after being picked up from nursery school by Riley and Jane. I asked her "Where's Daddy?" Alea looked up at me and said "Silly, Mommy, he's kissing Miss Jane in her house." She said it as though it was the most perfectly natural thing for her Daddy to do. I couldn't believe my ears. Surely, my little four-year-old daughter was mistaken.

I knew he spent time at Jane's house. She needed help with fixing "things" all the time. She even had called in the middle of the night and Riley went rushing over. That's what good friends and neighbors do... Right?

Jane was a drinker. She was often drunk and would get deeply depressed and threatened suicide on several occasions. I spent many hours talking her though an "episode." Riley had also helped her through tough times. They became drinking buddies. Almost every night he would stop over at her house to have a scotch. Then he would come home and we would share a bottle of wine – sometimes he would open a second bottle.

Of course, Riley denied that anything was going on between him and Jane. It was just the imagining of a small child and not to be taken seriously. I chose to believe him – once again. I closed my eyes and plowed ahead while that niggling little voice in the back of my head kept repeating... "Are you sure you want to get back on that roller coaster?" Instead of turning away, I bought a ticket and climbed back on board.

COME BACK TO ME

Riley's term of service on the new-born baby-boat was at an end. He met with his career counselors and was assured that he would be able to be transferred for shore-duty in his beloved California. We didn't know where, but most likely in San Diego. Of course, there are never any guarantees where you will be stationed, but just the possibility of going "home" were welcomed words.

We knew that it was a risk, but as Riley went off on his last deployment on board Baby Boat, I packed us up and moved us to California. We decided that no matter where Riley was stationed, we would have our home base be near my family in the San Francisco Bay area. If Riley were stationed in San Diego, he would stay on base for the week and come home on weekends. I truly felt this was the best scenario for everyone. There would be a cut in Riley's pay since he would not be going to sea and work opportunities were plentiful for me in San Francisco.

I didn't rush into getting a house or job right away. I spent a month with my parents and brothers and all the rest of the Logan family. I visited Riley's brother and his family. I reconnected and reacquainted myself. It was peaceful back here in the warmth and loving arms of the people that shared my heritage.

When the month was over, we were still four more months away from Riley's return from deployment and another month until he got his orders. I set out to find us a house.

It was the early 1980's and the housing market was doing some really strange things. I found a four-bedroom house perfect for our family and I was able to negotiate a lease-purchase agreement. We would finally have a "home of our own".

The house task was complete and I moved on to finding a job. I was quickly snatched up by a graphic arts firm as the head typographer. The pay was great. The benefits were great. I loved the owners and co-workers. Everything was coming together like a well-executed plan. Well… it was for me in California… but Connecticut… not so much.

Riley took leave immediately after the deployment and joined us in our new home in California. He was there for a little more than two weeks. We didn't want to use all his leave time before he got orders. But, those were the best two weeks we had had in a very long time.

We took the kids to the water park; had cook-outs with other family members; went to dinner at the restaurant where we had our first real date; and just enjoyed being together. We shared bottles of wine, but there wasn't a lot of heavy drinking. We just felt so very normal.

About a month after Riley returned to Connecticut, we expected him to get his orders. The wait would be over. We would know if our risk had paid off. I felt so sure that I would hear him say, "I'll be there in a few weeks." But, instead what I heard is that his orders were for him to run the electronics lab right where he was – Groton, Connecticut.

We made a huge mistake. We trusted the military to send us to a place where we would most likely not end up being assigned. How could we have been so stupid? If we had just taken a look around, we would have realized that we were using "fantasy land" thinking.

OK. Now we had to deal with the situation. We decided we would try the long-distance thing. It had not worked for us before because I kept anticipating an eminent move. This time I would settle in and not focus on joining him. We planned that Riley would come home for a week every three months. It was better than nothing. We thought we would find a way to work it all out.

Riley settled into the Chief's Quarters and I made our new house a home. I plunged head first into my job and so did he. We came home every three months, but it always felt that he was just a visitor. Each time he left, it was harder and harder for all of us. That was the way things were for almost a year.

In August, Riley came home and we had a huge birthday party for him. Everyone had a wonderful time. But... Riley didn't want to go back to Connecticut. He hesitated making the arrangements for his flight and didn't let me take him to the airport until the last minute. On the trip there, he asked if I would consider dropping everything and coming back to Connecticut. He said the reality is that he will probably never get stationed in California. That would mean us having to continue being a long-distance family for many more years. He asked me to please consider it if I wanted to keep us together.

So... I knew I heard the words, but I wasn't sure if I understood him correctly. It seemed he was saying that if I didn't move us back to Connecticut our relationship would be over. I knew he was unhappy about the situation, I just didn't know how unhappy he was.

When he called to let me know he had arrived back at the barracks safely, I asked him if what I thought he was saying was what he was actually saying. He said that he just couldn't go on this way – being together, but not being together. A decision had to be made and he didn't think he should be the one to make it.

Riley had taken a part-time job at the Chief's Club as a bartender. His day was full. Although Susan and Jim had been transferred to Virginia, they still kept in touch with Riley. There was a lot of attachment to the East Coast, and I wondered if there would ever be a time for us on the West Coast. I knew I was just California Dreamin'.

By mid-October, I started my plan in motion for moving the family (yet again) across country. Only a few people in my entire family and social circle were in favor of my decision. I had a gigantic yard sale, sold my lease option on the house, packed up my kids and headed for Connecticut It was two weeks from Thanksgiving and if I didn't get on the road now, I'd have a problem with the weather. So off we went.

NOW GO AWAY

I arrived in Groton on the Sunday before Thanksgiving. I found the cheapest motel room I could and spent almost all of my remaining money on a room. Riley joined us there the next morning. He took the day off so we could go house hunting. We decided on a cute little place just a few blocks from the beach. It was a "winter rental" so it was completely furnished and suited our needs perfectly.

Although Riley helped me pick out the house, he was not there when I signed the rental agreement and handed over the money Riley had given me to cover the rent and deposit. I wasn't concerned about the lack of money because Riley would have more when I picked him up from the base that evening. We planned on doing our grocery shopping on our way home.

It was Tuesday and the autumn chill was setting in. The leaves had long since turned red and orange and had fallen from the limbs of the tress. They were now in heaps in people's yards and along the roadside. I sat in my car and waited for Riley to come through the gate. I waited for more than two hours – where could he be?

A tap on my window startled me. I didn't recognize this person, but I rolled down the window and he handed me a note – "The Chief told me to give this to you." What? Huh? Where is he? But the man just turned and walked away.

I unfolded the paper and saw in neatly printed letters:

Linny – Must get away. Too close to the situation to figure this out. Need some space. Don't worry about money, I have plenty. I'll see you when I get back. -- Riley

What? I didn't understand. Away? Space? He had plenty of space when the kids and I were in California. If this was how he felt, why had I driven 3,000 miles because he wanted his family back? None of this made any sense to me. I was the one who needed to figure things out.

I still had a little money in my wallet. I stopped at the grocery store and managed to find something for dinner and breakfast. I went home and did some heavy thinking. Thanksgiving was just a day away and I had no money and no food.

The next morning, I called Travelers' Aid Society and they told me there would be a $20 food voucher for me at the local grocery store. They also directed me to the Town Hall and gave me the name of a woman who could help me. I picked up the food voucher and went to the Town Hall. The woman was very helpful and gave me another food voucher for another $20. She told me to come back on Monday, after the holiday, and she would provide me more assistance. Because it was Thanksgiving weekend, no one was in the office that could approve her requests.

I went to the store knowing I had only $40 for food that needed to last at least five days. It was difficult because I had no basic supplies – salt, sugar, etc. I bought a large chicken for our Thanksgiving dinner and added to it some other things that I thought would get us through. I was thinking – roast the chicken and use half of it for dinner, use the other half for a chicken casserole, and use anything left over for soup. I bought some hamburger and hot dogs and several boxes of mac 'n cheese.

The deli had end pieces that they set aside and have available for anyone asking. They were free and I asked for whatever they had.

Then I asked the butcher about bones that they had to give away. The butcher stressed that they were for dogs, but the bones he put into a plastic bag were still very meaty and had lots of morrow. They'd be perfect for soup if I added the deli roast beef to the pot.

Then I checked out the produce. There was a rack of various fresh vegetables that were reduced to nearly nothing. I picked through them to find the best looking veggies for the cheapest price. I asked the produce clerk, if they had anything that was about to go into the trash. He told me he had just put a box of them in the small dumpster behind the store.

I checked out and my total was just over $40, but the clerk told me not to worry about it. And told me she hoped that my Thanksgiving was good.

Before I headed home, I drove behind the store where I found a box sitting neatly on top of the dumpster. These veggies did not look old – in fact they were very fresh. Just then the clerk peeked out the door and gave me a wave. I knew he had put them there just for me. This box of lettuce, carrots, celery, peppers, potatoes and so many other things was a gift of love from a stranger.

I was in tears as I drove home. These people that lived in this town were good people. I don't know what I would have done if they had not been so generous. My tears were also fueled by my anger towards Riley. This was wrong on so many levels. I decided I would try to get enough money together to get home to the people who loved me most – my California family. In the back of my head I could hear the words – *"Are you sure you want to get back on that roller coaster ride?"*

I was determined to find out where Riley was. I called the boat and asked for Riley. I knew he wasn't there, but I was fishing for answers. I could tell the young man who answered was not experienced in dealing with wives looking for their husbands. The more seasoned sailors were programed to give pat answers such as: He just left. He's in the shower. He's not available. That was all code for he was not there and they didn't want to tell me where he was or exactly when he left. But, this young man gave me information that I would never have been given by anyone else. He told me Riley was on leave and the emergency phone number where he could be reached. *PAY DIRT!!* Riley was in New Hampshire which could only mean he was with the Rittenhouse family.

The phone in our new house was still operational from the last tenants. I dialed the number and asked for Riley. There was some shuffling and then a bit of silence. I could tell that someone was on the other end of the phone by the breathing. Then the voice of a little Asian girl came across the line. It was Riley doing his very poor imitation that he did every time we had Chinese food. When I told him to cut the crap, he hung up. I called back. These calls continued several times until a voice came on the phone telling me I was ruining their Thanksgiving and to stop calling. *What?? I was ruining their Thanksgiving??*

The weather was warm for the end of November, but the skies were overcast. The kids and I went down to the beach and ran in the surf of the chilly ocean waves. We threw sticks for the dog and drew pictures in the sand. Then we came home and played *Chutes and Ladders* and then *Sorry!* We watched TV and Alea waited for her Daddy. She was seven years old and was still a Daddy's girl.

"When will Daddy be here?" She would ask. Brian responded with "What do you care when he gets here? He's probably not coming. He doesn't care about us. I hope he never comes back."

I knew I would never forgive Riley for abandoning us on that weekend. But, I was a woman with two children and 3,000 miles away from anyone who truly cared about us. I had no money and no means of getting back home. I would have to work this to my advantage or I would find myself in a very precarious position. I knew I must use Riley to regain some financial security and then leave him cold and not look back.

Riley returned from New Hampshire and showed up on the doorstep with flowers and gifts. He walked in the house as if nothing had happened previously. I let him. I let him fall into our family routine. I needed his money, so I planned to use him and it started with me letting him back into the house. I had no idea that I was the main ingredient in a Frog Soup.

If you put a frog into a pot of boiling water, it will jump out immediately. If you put the frog in a pot of cold water and slowly bring the water to a boil – you'll end up with frog soup.

What I didn't realize was that by letting him back in I might slowly forgive him in an unspoken kind of way. I thought I was in control of everything and would not be duped again by his charm. But, it's a funny thing about charm… it can be mesmerizing.

HAPPY BIRTHDAY TO ME!

Our cute little house was in what was considered to be a touristy community. We were only blocks from the beach. There was a sizeable back yard that edged off into a creek. Tall trees, plants and shrubs lined the perimeter creating a natural fence and the rest of the yard was lawn.

I have no idea why, but Riley seemed to enjoy being out in the yard on Sunday, mowing the grass, trimming the shrubs, etc. Of course, he had always had a few drinks before he got out there.

There comes a time in the fall when the lawn gets mowed for the last time before the frost and snow sets in. It just so happened that on my birthday the lawn would be mowed for the last time that season. Riley had been celebrating my birthday quite a bit that day, so I was a little worried when he insisted he MUST do the lawn on my birthday.

I'm not sure what I was doing, but I wasn't paying much attention to whatever was going in the backyard. It may have been the anniversary of my birth, but there was still laundry, rooms to clean, and dinner to cook. If I was lucky, we could all sit down and watch the football game.

It seemed that Riley was taking a lot longer on the yard than his normal lawn chore day. Oh well, I was busy and as long as he was in the yard, I knew where he was and what he was doing. I wasn't too concerned.

I had just make a big bowl of popcorn and put out chips and dips for the football game, when Riley came in and said I need to inspect what he had done. He was all giggly and excited for me to view his handiwork. He had never done that before. Something was up. He told me to close my eyes and took me out into the yard. Then he said – "OK! Open 'em"!

It took me a minute to understand the whole concept of what he had done. I was a mix of delight and horror. This would not be good at the spring thaw.

A giant birthday card had been carved into the grass in the yard! HAPPY BIRTHDAY on one line and LINNY on the next and then a "heart" underneath my name and it was outlined with wavy lines all around. I was amazed at his creativity – because generally Riley was not. The difference in the grass height was a good three inches. The letters were almost down to the bare ground. I was laughing and hugging him. He was so proud of himself. I didn't see him like that very often, so I put my negativity aside and joined in his glee. This was a good birthday.

The following weekend was the first snowfall of the season. I stepped out onto our back deck to see the white outlines of branches of what was once leaf shrouded branches. My eyes looked at the yard and saw HAPPY BIRTHDAY LINNY outlined in snow. It would take another snowfall to cover the greeting. I smiled, but I knew the grass cut so close to the ground may not survive the cold. Those words might stay in that lawn for several seasons.

I had made a promise to myself not to let the charmer mesmerize his way back into my heart. But, for him to go so far out of his comfort zone by a being creative and letting the world know of his feelings, well… that was too much for me to resist. During the two years we had been in that house, he was almost the husband that I wanted. He was making an effort to make me feel secure and loved. There were exceptions – there was an affair – but it seemed that was over and his family was his focus.

It was also during this time that his drinking was really ramping up. I rationalized that he had a part-time job as a bartender; of course he would be drinking more. Besides, there were still the command parties and social events. There was booze all around us, every day and at all times. It seemed there was always a drink in Riley's hand. But, I thought to myself, isn't this the way it is for all Navy families?

In reality it was just another ingredient in my Frog Soup.

DEAR RILEY

Just before being transfer to the next duty station, Riley and I decided to take a huge leap of faith and legalize our relationship by getting married. It was a simple ceremony in front of a Justice of the Peace. Brian and Alea stood next to us as their parents committed themselves to love, honor and cherish until death do us part. It didn't feel romantic. It was just a formalization of how things had been. Being married would simplify our lives as far as the Navy was concerned. It was a matter of practicality.

A few years later, we were transferred back to Virginia to a sea-going submarine. Riley was deployed when the movers delivered our belonging and I began the task of unpacking and setting up our household. Both Brian and Alea were unpacking their boxes as though it were Christmas in May.

I was working on the boxes marked as "Master". I hung up and folded away all the clothes. I organized the shoes. I was proud that I had accomplished so much in just a short period of time. Then I found a box filled with Riley's things from his dresser. I carefully put things away. At the bottom of the box there was a bulging brown envelope stuffed with letters. A few fell out that were from me to him when he had been at sea way back when we were first together in Norfolk.

"How sweet is that? He saved all my letters." Inside I was filled with warm contentment as I put the letters back into the torn envelope. But, then I saw handwriting that was not mine. There were letters from other people. Who were these people? Some were postmarked while we were in Connecticut.

I sat in the middle of the bedroom floor surrounded by my husband's infidelity. There were letters from his ex-wife and Jane, Darlene and some chick named Candy. What kind of name was that – Candy. All the letters described in detail their intimate encounters and the love they each felt for Riley. Jane wrote about how exciting it was that they took so many risks in their encounters. She told of an instance when she called in the middle of the night and they had sex in her bedroom just on the other side of the wall separated her bedroom from ours. The warm contentment I had felt just an hour before rapidly turned into disbelief and pain.

Now what? Riley was at sea and unavailable. I could not confront him. And if I had – what would I do after he tried to convince me it was nothing.

I called Carrot. We talked for hours and explored all my options. My children loved Riley. Alea never knew any other father and Riley claimed her as his own. Riley would be gone more than 50% of the time while he was at this four-year duty assignment. Financially, I was secure and was able to give my children a good life.

I replaced the letters into the folder and placed it under Riley's sweaters in his bottom dresser drawer. He would know I had looked at them, because how could I not when I had to put them away? I also wrote to him and told him I had found and read the letters. I made no threats. I only told him the facts.

His response letter was angry that I had read his mail. He wrote – "Don't ever open or read my mail again." That was the entire letter. My response was "Don't ever have mail or letters in my house that you don't want me to read." That was my entire letter. After that everything went back to the way it was – sort of.

MAYBE IT'S JUST ME

Maybe the problem wasn't really Riley. Maybe I should change myself and be the woman he wanted. I went on a diet and became an exercise fanatic. I went to a therapist to find out how to "fix" myself. I changed my hair color, my make-up, my clothing style. If I could be a different woman when he got home, maybe he wouldn't stray.

I was so excited when he returned from sea. I stood on the pier with Brian and Alea and watched him climb down the gangway. The kids ran to him. He came over and gave me a hug. He told me he liked the new look. We never spoke of the letters again. We went home and had a wonderful family evening.

The next night, Riley went to the store to get bread and milk. But he disappeared and was gone for two days. There were no phone calls. There was nothing that let me know he was OK or when he would be home. He simply disappeared. But on the third day, I got this phone call.

Riley: I'm lost. Come get me please.

Linda: Where are you?

Riley: I think I'm in Atlantic Beach. Oh yeah... I'm in Atlantic Beach.

Linda: Where's your car?

Riley: That woman must have it.

Linda: What woman?

Riley: I'm not sure. I was at her house.

Linda: What's the last thing you remember?

Riley: The party.

Linda: What party? Where was it?

Riley: At that restaurant. You know.

Linda: No I don't know. Where was the woman's house?

Riley: I'm not sure. There was a hotel close by.

Linda: Where are you calling from?

Riley: A drug store.

Linda: So what do you want me to do?

Riley: I want you come get me and help me find my car.

Linda: Why should I do that?

Riley: Because you have a car and I can't find mine.

Linda: I ***know*** where my car is and I ***know*** where I was last night. You're almost 50 miles from home. I suggest you find a policeman and tell him you've lost your car. Maybe they can help you. I cannot come to Atlantic Beach to get you.

Everyone knows that the front seat on the roller coaster is the scariest. I knew I was in that seat. I knew that my marriage was never going to be happily ever after. I knew I would have to find ways to make it work, but that I was married to a man who wasn't totally committed to our marriage. I knew nothing had ever really changed from the vanilla wafers to now. The apple strudel was just a figment of my imagination.

I finally climbed out of the frog soup pot. I was amazed that I had let things get to this point. How long had it been since that awful Thanksgiving – three years? Had I forgotten how awful it really was? I seemed to have let myself get caught up in the romance of the last few years. Riley had managed to charm me back into what I thought was a viable loving relationship. He was good at that. He was good at convincing me he was a different man than he really was. Reality was knocking on my noggin. It was time for me to see things as they really were.

Now that my blinders were off, I started to recognize that Riley was drinking a lot more than I realized. It was a bottle of wine every night with dinner after 3 or 4 scotch drinks the minute he got home from work. He seemed to get drunk every weekend. I thought back at how many times we had argued over his drinking. I always ended up feeling like I was a bitch. But even if I was, it didn't mean he didn't have a drinking problem. I thought back over all the inconsistencies, his wanting his family and then rejecting us, his inability to stay monogamous. I wondered how much of it had been influenced by his alcohol consumption. Having never been exposed to alcoholism, I wasn't really sure what I was looking at as I examined my past Riley experiences.

REHAB VIRGINITY

I was working at the shipyard managing a small office that produced technical drawings and blueprints. It wasn't very exciting. There was no creativity. It was just a job. The worker that I supervised was the granddaughter of one of the members of the executive staff. She was a spoiled brat named Victoria and I had difficulty trying to get her to do a solid day's work. I was very unhappy and just really hated that job.

The shipyard job was good money and we needed that. It seemed there was never enough to get us through the month. I stuck to a strict budget and it just seemed that the money disappeared before all the bills were paid. I was so frustrated with the financial situation, that I considered getting a second job.

Riley's boat was in port most of the time, so he was home almost every night. But it was a long commute from our house in Williamsburg to his pier in Norfolk. We decided that as much as we loved the house we were in and as much as we didn't want the kids to change schools – again – we put our names on the list for Navy housing.

It would mean saving the money it cost for Riley's commute and a huge reduction in our housing costs. It was a good move and we looked forward to the change. I was hoping it would help me get a handle on the money and we just might be able to save to buy a house.

Riley came home one day and didn't fix himself a drink. He had something he had to talk to me about and I listened closely. His commanding officer had issued him orders to participate in a new program. He was to report to the Navy Alcohol and Rehabilitation

Program the following Monday. We didn't know anything about this program and I wasn't so sure Riley needed to be ordered to go to this place. Riley told me he would be going to an interview and if it was determined that he might be a problem drinker, he would have to stay there as an inpatient.

Well, it was Thursday now and he didn't report until Monday. So he just wouldn't drink between now and then and he would show that he didn't need their help to stop drinking because drinking was not a real problem for him. It was just something he did. Riley and I thought he'd be back on board his sub by the following Tuesday.

But, there was more to this program. If it were determined that Riley needed to be admitted, I would also have to take part. What?? I had a job and a family and I wasn't a drinker, so why would I want to do that. Riley told me it wasn't about my drinking or about me at all – it was the rules of the program. If I didn't attend classes, he might just be dishonorably discharged. Well, I guess that means I'd be going to Norfolk for a day or two.

When I returned to work the next day, I was told that my services were no longer needed. I wanted to be upset, but I just couldn't manage it. I was elated to be away from the little disrespectful demon seed that had been a thorn in my side for the past year. Besides, if I was going to have to go to Norfolk every day, I didn't need to be worrying about my job.

It was Monday. Riley had gone to be interviewed at the alcohol treatment center (ARC). I expected he would be home early and we could have an early dinner. But, instead, I got a phone call asking me to pack him some clothes and bring them to Norfolk. He would be staying at the center for the next six weeks or longer. I was surprised. Riley had not had a drink for almost a week. Surely that meant he did not need to go to rehab.

I packed him a bag and dutifully took it to the center. When I got there, the contents were dumped onto a table and inspected for hidden bottles of booze. Certain items were removed, like his aftershave and mouthwash. These items were put into a bag and I was told I could take them back home after my meeting with the counselor. I went through the motions and followed the directions, but I was sure I would just be going home and waiting for Riley to finish his program.

I was introduced to Gill who would be my counselor/moderator for all my activities while I was at the center. I was to be there at 8 a.m. the next morning to start my rehabilitation. I was shocked. Rehabilitation??? Me???? I was not a drinker and I did not have a problem with alcohol. But, they held the keys to Riley's career and in that, my future as well. I would be a good little wife and do as I was told.

The first few days, I listened and didn't really have much to say. I let everyone else do the talking. My group was all women, all wives of patients. It was discovered that a few of them were alcoholics and were transferred to a non-military rehab center. It seemed to me these women had problems far worse than mine. While I was being sympathetic and sad for them, Cheryl entered our group.

Cheryl and Mark were familiar faces. He was a shipmate of Riley's and Cheryl was his wife. I would never have imagined that they would need to be here. Mark was on track to become a Naval officer and Cheryl was a stay-at-home mother of two. They always gave me the impression of having all their eggs in one basket and knowing where the basket was at all times.

I suppose it was because we knew each other that we became buddies in our group. We ate lunch together and went to Al-Anon meetings together.

Riley was working on his own stuff and occasionally, bits and pieces were funneled back to me. I was learning something new every day. The more I learned about alcoholism, the more I knew that we were both exactly where we needed to be. Finally, I had come to terms with the fact that Riley was absolutely an alcoholic. Of course my next question was how I could get him to stop or how had I helped make him become an alcoholic.

As I sat listening and learning, I recalled an incident that had taken place just a month or so before Riley entered rehab. I was surprised that I was willing to share this event because it was embarrassing. I didn't need to be told that it was dysfunctional to know that it was just an insane solution to a very large problem.

In an effort to keep Riley from leaving the house when I knew he wanted to go get more booze, I let the air out of his tires. It was close to midnight and I didn't think anyone would be able to see. My plan was to discover it before Riley and then tell him that he has a tire that needs to be replaced.

What sane person deflates car tires to keep their spouse from drinking? Imagine being in your driveway in the middle of night, dressed in a flannel nightgown (although it would have been better if I had been in a sexy piece of lingerie with those fuzzy topped high-heel slides), and you're hunched down manipulating the tire valve. At that time the friendly neighborhood watch sees something suspicious. The watchperson doesn't realize it's you – the long-time resident and neighbor.

Watchperson: Hey there!! What are you doing?

Me: Who??? Me??

Watchperson: Yeah!! YOU!!

Me:	Well... I just...
Watchperson:	Oh! It's you, Ms Riley... Are you OK?
Me:	Ummm... well... yes... I was just trying to... ummm...
Watchperson:	Is your car OK? Did someone mess with it? Looks like the tires have been flattened.
Me:	Well... no they're fine...
Watchperson:	Do you know who did that?? Let's fill out a report. I'll just get my clipboard.
Me:	Oh no... that's OK...
Watchperson:	Now... when did you notice the vandalism??
Me:	No... no... I uhhh... I like them that way.
Watchperson:	What?? (as he cocks his head in confusion)

As I walked back inside the house, I thought; that didn't go so well. Maybe I should re-think that plan. Maybe I should just eliminate it from my repository of ways to prevent Riley from getting to the liquor store.

NOT MY FAULT

I learned all those things Al-Anon teaches, but I learned it straight forward and clearly explained. I didn't have to figure it out for myself; like we have to if you just go to meetings. I learned it in the group sessions. There was nothing I could do to stop him. There was nothing I had done to make him an alcoholic.

Some of the terms fit our family perfectly. We were dysfunctional. By this time, Brian was getting into little troublesome situations and Alea was almost uncontrollable for a child at the age of 12. I never had equated any of that to Riley's drinking. But, I learned that the kids' behavior and my depression, added to our financial problems, had a lot to do with alcoholism.

Beside group therapy, they had classes on how the brain works and what happens to the body when the alcohol passes the lips. We saw the movies "Lost Weekend" and "Days of Wine and Roses." We learned about what can happen to the body if the alcoholism continues. I compiled binders full of printed information. I bought books and I attended Al-Anon every evening.

It was a four-week program and I soaked up all the information I could during those four weeks. Even though group sessions ended, the women in the group stayed close. We went to meetings together and visited each other. We became a sisterhood.

While I was still doing the group thing, we were assigned a unit in Navy housing. I was delighted and made the move in between group sessions. Riley would come home to a new house and a fresh start at a new life. Maybe this was the chance for our marriage to be renewed.

Two weeks later he came home. For the first time in a long time, I felt appreciated and loved. I felt I could trust him again. We were on a bit of a honeymoon and I was enjoying every second.

The center of our lives was AA and Al-Anon. Social events and friendships were all non-alcoholic. Our friends were all recovering as we were. The friends we had before seemed to disappear from our life. I was OK with that. I was happy to have my husband back and willing to make sacrifices to keep him healthy and sane.

We seldom went to meetings at the same locations. Riley would go his way and I would go mine. We each had our favorite meetings and would usually meet up afterwards at a coffee shop for a snack before heading home. We called it the meeting after the meeting with seldom less than six people gathered in a booth.

That was a very good year for the Riley family.

THEY BITE?

Alea was not an easy child. Her pre-teen years were not any easier. But a parent knows when her unruly off-spring is just being cantankerous and when they are in trouble. I suspected something was really wrong with my daughter. She was missing a lot of school because she was having headaches. At first they were just an irritation, but eventually they would be the cause of several trips to the emergency room.

She would insist that the lights be off in the examining room until the medical personnel would enter and they she would cry from the brightness of the light. It hurt more when she was lying down than when she was sitting up – so she stayed in a sitting or reclining position. Blood tests were taken, but everything appeared normal. Each time she was released and told to just get through them.

On our third visit to the hospital, Alea was examined from head to toe by a pediatrician. Every inch of her body was inspected. What the doctor discovered was shocking. There was a spot on her upper inner thigh, just above the back of her knee that had an angry looking sore. It was about an inch in diameter and looked like a crater filled with a very unpleasant sea of puss. That was it! That was what was causing the problems.

Alea told the doctor she had been bit by something when we were at a cookout a couple of weeks prior. She thought it would just go away and didn't pay much attention to it. She said she washed it, but it got bigger.

The bite was from a centipede. I didn't even know they would bite and I certainly didn't know they were poisonous. Now that we knew the cause, regimens of medications were prescribed and a course of treatment began.

Sleep was nearly impossible for her. Each time she would fall asleep, she would end up lying flat and the pain would increase. Riley and I took turns getting up and calming her when she woke up screaming in the middle of the night.

One morning I woke up terrified because I had slept through the entire night. I was afraid Alea had died because she did not wake me up. There was no screaming and no calling for me. It had just been a peaceful, restful night. I rushed to her room.

I couldn't believe my eyes. Riley was on Alea's bed. He was sitting up with his back against the wall and he was asleep. Alea was beside him and leaning her back against his chest so she was reclining against him. She was also asleep. He must have been there almost the entire night.

I made the coffee and it wasn't long before I heard him whisper for me as I walked by Alea's room. He asked if I could slip a pillow or two under Alea so he could get off the bed. We maneuvered the pillows so that she was propped up. As he slipped from under her, she mumbled… "Daddy?" Riley kissed her forehead and told her he would be right back. She fell back to sleep and finally seemed to be pain free.

After that, Riley and I alternated "sleeping duty" throughout the night. But, it seemed she was getting better faster now and it was only about a week until she was back to being the precocious, sassy twelve-year old that she had been before the hungry centipede tasted her flesh.

The drunken Riley would never have been so dedicated to taking care of a sick child. He would never have sacrificed a night of booze and womanizing for the opportunity to provide comfort and support to anyone – not even Alea. I was grateful that the Riley in my presence. At that time Riley was the man I always knew he could be.

WHAT'S A FEW MORE YEARS

Riley was getting home from work later. He was preparing to be transferred back to a sea-going submarine and had to jump through some hoops to make it happen. After work he would go to a meeting. I didn't see him except at breakfast and dinner. Other than that, he was not home. It was OK because he was not drinking. I reasoned with myself that his sobriety must be his top priority. I could not stand in the way of that just because I felt a little neglected.

One evening, Riley pulled in the driveway and went straight to bed. I was just cleaning up before I joined him there. There was something going on outside and I opened the door to find two women talking to each other on my front stoop.

"Can I help you?" I asked.

"No. We want to talk to Riley."

"What do you want with my husband?" I asked.

"We want to talk to him."

"What do you want to talk to him about?" They weren't answering my questions and I was getting angry.

"I said I want to talk to him. I'm coming in."

"NO! You're not coming in. What do you want?" I pressed.

"Just tell him that I don't want to see him anymore. Keep him away from me!"

With that, both women turned on their heels and went back to their car. But, I watched from the bathroom window and they only went to the corner where they parked the car and turned off the headlights.

Riley was in the bedroom pretending to have slept through the whole thing. I pushed at him and told him the coast was clear, he could come out now. He denied any knowledge of who the women were or why they would want to confront him. He said they must have had the wrong house.

Oh! Really! How many sailors in Navy housing do you think have the name of Riley? I knew it was hopeless to try to get him to confess, but in my heart I knew. It didn't matter if he was drinking or not. He was a womanizing son-of-a-bitch.

Something happened to me as a result of that realization. After 15 years of being with Riley, I was now no longer in a honeymoon haze. My eyes were open and I made the decision that I needed to stay married, even if I wasn't feeling that my marriage was valid. I hadn't been working and had no money for an escape. It seemed like all the traumatic encounters with Riley-created chaos always took place when I was in the position of being extremely dependent on his income. It also was clear that my kids needed continuity. Brian would be graduating in just a couple of years and three years after that it would be Alea's graduation. I needed to stay with Riley for five more years, and then I could leave and do whatever I wanted.

I wouldn't be leaving Riley because of his drinking. I would be leaving because of his inability to keep his penis safely zipped in his pants. I was leaving him because he had no intention of being a faithful husband. During my days in group I learned how alcohol promotes a lack of morals, but Riley was sober. Alcohol had nothing to do with the fact he was screwing around.

I didn't tell Riley I was leaving him in five years. Instead I asked him if he would ever be monogamous. His answer was no. He couldn't and wouldn't stop having sex with other women. I asked if he wanted to end our marriage. He said no to that also. He enjoyed being a part of our little family and it provided him an image of stability. He needed that especially since he went through rehab. If his personal life appeared to be falling apart, he might be put under the alcoholism microscope of the Navy. His career would be over.

I agreed to stay with him under certain conditions. We would continue as a family and present a united front. We would buy a house in which I could become settled and secure. When he retired from the Navy he would take a civilian job and he would make the house payment from his retirement pay. He could live anywhere he wanted. It was his choice. But he would always make the house payment.

There was more… We will have separate rooms and I will never share a bed with him again. We would put together a budget that paid off both our cars and by the time he retired I would be able to keep up the house expenses as long as he made the mortgage payment. There would be no divorce because I did not want to lose my military benefits.

Riley agreed. I think he felt he was getting the best end of the stick since I was allowing him the image he needed to stay in the Navy.

A HOME OF OUR OWN

Riley's sub went to sea a couple of months later and I had full power of attorney. I found a house and had us moved in before he ever returned from deployment.

The house was nothing very fancy. Just a brick rancher, four bedrooms and two baths, den and screened in back porch. The backyard was huge. The garage had been converted to a den with a giant-sized fireplace. It wasn't a house you would find in Architectural Digest, but it felt like home to me. I knew I could live here for the rest of my life. I knew this would be a home where my grandchildren (when I had some) would be happy to visit me. It was practical and suited me just fine.

Riley returned from deployment and told me he loved the house. The payments were reasonable and when I reminded him of our "arrangement" he told me this would not be a problem. He was approaching his 23rd year of military service and had decided to delay retirement until he had 30 years. That would give us seven solid years of mortgage payments before retirement.

I was working for as an office manager for a real estate company full time. But, I wanted to make some extra money so I took an additional full-time job at the local newspaper working nights as an obit writer. I worked weekends and three other nights, so I took on a job selling women's lingerie on my two available nights. I wanted to get the cars paid off and pay ahead on the mortgage.

REFUSAL TO RESCUE

Since I was gone from home so much, I didn't pay much attention to what Riley was doing. I would soon discover that he was back to the bottle and things were going downhill very quickly. He went back into ARC for a brief "refresher" and to help him get back on track with AA. Unfortunately, it didn't work because he was back to the bottle just days after being discharged.

I don't know how, but Riley was still managing to hold onto his career. He was dodging the bullets and it was just a matter of time before he got hit in the head.

I knew how bad things were with his drinking. I also thought that I would not intervene to try to stop him because he needed to hit his bottom. I had learned this in group at ARC and the lessons stuck with me. I took care of myself, the house and the kids, but I did not take care of Riley or come to his rescue.

"Mrs. Riley, we have your husband here." I had had these calls before and I knew the drill. It was the desk sergeant at the police department. They always called when Riley was picked up drunk in public.

"Would you please come pick him up?" asked the officer.

"No. I won't come get him." I responded.

"Well… he's just drunk and we really don't want to have to keep him here. So, why don't you just come get him?" he urged me.

"Riley got drunk by his own volition. I had nothing to do with it. I won't be punished by having to leave my warm bed and my warm house to come take him off your hands." I said firmly.

"What do you want US to do with him?" he seemed surprised at my refusal.

"Do what you do with all the other drunks." I told him.

"Aw, com' on! He's a really nice guy." I thought the officer was begging me to take Riley home.

"Yes." I agreed. "He's a really nice guy who is a drunk. It's a good thing he was not driving, huh? Good night, officer."

It was a familiar call. The officer knew Riley. He had been picked up for being drunk in public, indecent exposure, and making unwanted advances to a woman in a bar. He had become a familiar sight at the police station on Saturday nights in our community. Each time he was picked up, I would receive a phone call to come get him. Each time I refused. I refused to rescue him from his own consequences.

RISKY BUSINESS

I loved working at the newspaper. It gave me an outlet for my need to write. I had started many personal stories and a book about my childhood, but I could never go as far as I needed or make things cohesively jell. At first it was only obits – straight forward and factual. Then I petitioned to add obits that told a story of something significant that the deceased had accomplished in his life.

It was 1 a.m. and I was on my way out of the work building and going home. There had been a lot of activity that evening and I was ready for a bath and bed. I searched around the parking lot because I couldn't remember where I parked my car. I looked everywhere, but it was not there.

I went to the guard shack to report my car stolen. But, the guard told me the car had been repo'd. WHAT?? I had paid my car off and there was no loan, so how could it be repo'd? There had to be some kind of mistake. But, at that time on a snowy morning, I would get no answers. A co-worker took me home.

The next morning, I called the bank that had financed my car. The loan manager concurred that the car had, in fact, been paid off. They had not initiated a repossession.

I called the towing company and found out the repo had been by an independent finance company. In order to get the car back I would have to contact the finance company. And so that's what I did.

What I learned was pretty shocking to me. The car was actually in Riley's name. It was one of those little things that I never thought too much about. I don't even remember why we did it that way, but I knew that was true. Riley had taken out a loan using the car as collateral. The agreement was dated only weeks after the bank loan had been paid.

I confronted Riley and he matter-of-factly told me that it was correct that he had taken out the loan. He said he needed the money to pay off some debts to crew members. Since the car was in his name, he felt it unnecessary to tell me about it.

When I reminded him that he had his own car that he could have used for the loan, his reply was that he needed his car to get him back and forth to work and couldn't risk losing it. *HE COULDN'T TAKE THE RISK!!!* I was reeling with anger. I found myself screaming at him for being such a selfish ass. He calmly asked "Can you hear yourself? I can't listen to you when you are crazy like this." And he walked out the door and didn't return for several days.

I bought a car with my own credit and put it in just my name. I saw the whole experience as a lesson that I would not repeat. I could no longer trust Riley as being a financial partner. That worried me because the house was also in both our names. But, I knew he could never pay off or re-finance the house without my knowledge. I felt fairly secure with the mortgage situation.

Riley had almost three months of leave on his books. The command didn't like having that much and always encouraged the crew members to take their leave in large chunks when it got that high. Riley came home one evening and told me he was going on leave. That didn't mean much to me, except that he would be gone most of the time. He would be out drinking and carrying on. It was OK. I didn't really care. If I had still felt as though I was his wife, I would have cared. But, I had stopped caring a while back.

Our mortgage was paid by an allotment from Riley's paycheck. It was an excellent way to pay because I never had to think about making the payment. It was just automatically done for me. But, into the third month of Riley's vacation leave, I got a late notice from the bank. Our payment had not been made that month.

Of course, I called the bank. I was informed that no allotment had come on the first of the month, as it usually did. They informed me of how much it would cost to make the payment when late fees were added in. I was sure there had been some kind of mistake and told them I would call them back.

I talked to Riley. I asked for an explanation and told him he had to call the finance office on the base and get this taken care of. Instead of agreeing, he made a startling revelation.

It was the summer of 1989 and Riley told me he didn't have to go to work anymore. He was retired. I was dismayed, but not really surprised when I discovered that after numerous warnings, Riley was forced into retirement. Riley needed approval to re-enlist in order to reach his 30-year retirement point. His commanding officer felt Riley would not be able to stay out of trouble for those next four years and refused to sign the approval papers. The commanding officer actually did Riley a favor by allowing him to retire because if he had severely screwed up after re-enlisting, he would have lost his retirement pay and just been dishonorably discharged.

Riley had not told me of the retirement because he knew I would be worried and upset. He told me he knew it would be difficult, but we could get through this. Riley's friend, Jim Rittenhouse, had set Riley up with an excellent job with an excellent salary. We could actually pay ahead on the mortgage and within a few years, the house could be refinanced allowing me to manage the mortgage without Riley's income. Riley's loss of his Navy job could be a blessing in disguise.

And – oh by the way – he had a paper he needed me to sign. He wanted me to agree to rejecting the Survivor Benefit Plan which would provide me with half of Riley's retirement pay should he precede me in death. *Is he kidding me???* There was no way I was going to sign that paper.

RECOVERING WORKAHOLIC

I had quit my job at the real estate agency when I was offered a day job at the newspaper. I was writing community interest stories and I loved it. I quit the lingerie business and took on a part-time job at a fabric store. I was writing and working with other people who liked to sew and do crafts. It was hard work and I was tired all the time. But, I was in my element. Even though Riley was drinking, I loved my life.

Riley had a long commute to work and I often worried about him getting there and back. I imagined he may be driving drunk, but I wasn't sure what I should or could do about it.

One day, Riley didn't return home from work and I got worried. It was almost 10 pm when I called Jim and asked if he knew what time Riley left the office.

"Linda, Riley was fired today. He had been coming in late and leaving early every day. When he was there, he was making long distance calls and staying on the phone for hours. He left the office right after he arrived at 10 a.m. He's drinking is out of control – long lunches with him coming back drunk and nodding off at his desk. I don't know where he is, but I can no longer help him." Jim was apologetic, but informative.

The next morning, Riley was in the den with his coffee cup in hand. I told him I knew about his being fired. He responded with he wasn't fired; he just didn't want to work there anymore. In fact, he didn't want to work at all. He was retired and he planned on doing just that – retiring. He wanted to stop being a workaholic and just do whatever he wanted as long as it was not work.

In my mind, I had 30 days to figure out what I was going to do. If Riley wasn't going to work, I wasn't sure if I could financially afford to pay the mortgage, car payments and household expenses. Riley's retirement check would just barely cover the mortgage. Something was going to have to give.

Back before direct deposit, we all received our paychecks as paper checks and then deposited them into our bank accounts. Riley would often get his check in the mail and I was lucky if even half of it ended up in the bank. I was sinking. The house went into foreclosure. We didn't have enough equity to be able to refinance. In the end we lost the house and Riley's car. I had to come up with a new plan.

I was fortunate that Brian and Alea were no longer living at home. They had moved into their own places and Alea had given me my first grandchild. They would be OK. I was grateful for that. I suggested to Riley that he might want to find a place of his own. He moved in with another couple that he had met at a bar. It was just me now. I had to take care of myself on my own. It wasn't like I hadn't done that before, it was just that I was sad to have lost so much when I had invested so much over the past 20+years.

I found an apartment and began a new life.

Riley had moved into a house with a couple in his age group. Lilly and Jack were also alcoholics without any visible means of financial support. There was money coming from somewhere, but the source was unclear. There were rumors of Riley having an affair with Lilly and various other females who frequently visited.

It appeared that Riley now had everything he ever wanted. No job. No responsibility. No commitments. Free flowing alcohol. Revolving door to his bedroom. He was in alcoholism heaven.

My job at the newspaper was turning into a career. I had been chosen to write community stories for one of the newspapers bureau locations. This was my opportunity to shine. My first piece was on the issue of spousal abuse. It was a hit and I went on to write other stories of the human struggles in life.

Brian had taken a job in California working with the same company as my brother, Charlie. He was happy to be back with his cousins. He was with his family and out of the alcoholic chaos of his childhood. I missed him very much, but was happy he had found himself a place where he truly fit.

I was excited for Brian. His new job had him travelling the world. He would be spending five years in Hong Kong and after that — well — who knows where he would go!?!

Alea gave me a beautiful grandson and he was perfect in every way. I spoiled him in as much and as often as possibly could.

Christmas of 1992 was very difficult for the family. With Brian in California and Riley with his new people, we were on our own. The only thing we wanted was for baby Ryan to have a fantastic Christmas.

Alea was a single mom. She worked hard and barely made ends meet. She shared an apartment with a childhood friend and it seemed to be working as well as most roommate relationships went. She received no child support from Ryan's father. She was stubborn, independent and determined to do it all on her own. That is — unless her independence meant Ryan would not have something important.

Christmas was important. Alea had money for the necessities, but that didn't include big Santa gifts or even a Christmas tree. Much like her parents in 1972, she was a young family on a very strict budget.

Alea invited Riley to her home often. She still wanted that Daddy with the handlebar moustache, but he was long gone. Whenever Riley knew there would be young female friends visiting Alea, he always showed up. He would focus his attention on the young women. They teased him and tolerated him. When his passes were turned down often enough, he would be off again to someplace else that held more sexual possibilities.

I didn't have a lot of money. My job at the newspaper didn't pay a lot and I only survived because of my job at the fabric shop. I was barely making ends meet.

I had managed to get a new car and gave the older one to Alea. It was to be part of her Christmas present. I bought the Christmas tree, stocking stuffers and the food for Christmas dinner – which was to be held at Alea's. I also managed to buy Ryan some clothes to be used as gifts. And I had a heart to heart talk with Riley. I asked him what he planned to give Ryan. He said he would get whatever I thought was best. I told him toys. We needed to get him a Santa gift and some other toys. I told him to plan to spend about $100. I told him not to worry about Alea, all she wanted for Christmas was for Ryan to have a great day.

Two days before Christmas, I called Riley and asked if he wanted me to wrap any of Ryan's gifts. He said he would bring them over. When asked what he got for him, he rattled off different toys. I thought, oh, that's nice. He really listened to me. But, the next day – Christmas Eve – when I called again about the gifts, he told me he didn't have any. He said someone had taken them out of the truck. And he didn't have any money to buy any gifts.

His past behavior was always to present the image that he was thoughtful, caring, and responsible and the rest of the world was all ridiculous. In my heart, I know there had never been any gifts bought. I knew he had other plans for his money. I knew he needed to buy gifts for his girlfriend and roommates and their families. His real family didn't stand a chance.

But, Ryan had a wonderful Christmas morning because Alea's friends pulled together and they bought him several great gifts. Several of my friends also chipped in. The little guy was happy. He played and played and Alea and I watched him with tears in our eyes. We had the best gift ever. We had Ryan.

Riley showed up for dinner and Alea was cordial. He brought with him a box of candy for me and a box for Alea. He had nothing for Ryan. He left very early – right after dinner – because he said he had other gifts to deliver.

I don't know what happened to the man I spent Christmas with in 1972. The alcohol pod people must have taken him while he was passed out after a stupor. As much as I had loved him in 1972, I hated him in 1992.

PART FOUR

GO WEST DEAR WOMAN

Both of my kids had decided to return to their home state of California. I wasn't ready yet. I had a job I loved and lots of friends. My life was full and I didn't want to leave it to go back to start over again, even if it was my home.

At Christmas in 1993, Brian called to wish me a Merry Christmas and to let me know that my father was very ill. He said I should really consider coming back home. I told him I didn't have enough money to take that kind of vacation. He explained that a vacation was not what he meant. He wanted me to move back to California. I told him I would think about it.

A few hours later, I got a similar call from Alea. "Please come home, Mom. Granddad needs you. We all need you."

I made a few more calls, to my brothers and to my mother. I talked to Daddy, but did not tell him I knew he was sick. I had no idea how I would manage to get back to California or if I should just take a short trip there. But, I couldn't do both – it had to be one or the other.

I talked to my editors and they told me there would always be another job, another story, another newspaper. They would help me try to find something in California. One editor told me – you only have one father and your family is already out there. Whatever was keeping me in Virginia was something not as important as my family. It was time to let go of any imaginary ties on the east coast and migrate west.

I had a good friend at the fabric shop named Mary. She and her husband sat down with me and we came up with a plan. Yet another plan! My life was filled with plans!

Riley had an income and could easily be manipulated. He was constantly drinking, but still most of his money was being given away to his drinking friends. Mary said maybe I should be getting some of that gifted money. Riley and I were still talking, still friendly, still married. I would convince Riley that he wanted to come to California with me. He could visit his brother and then return to Virginia by himself. He would travel with me in my car and just "help" me get there. He eagerly agreed.

We loaded up a trailer and arrived in California two weeks later. Riley minimized his drinking during the trip and we actually had a pleasant time.

We stayed with my parents and I started working for a newspaper that required a two-hour commute. The newspaper job didn't last long. I quit after only a few weeks and took a job with Amtrak out of San Francisco. My father was so happy when I took that job. He was very proud to have a "railroad" person in the family.

Eighteen months after I arrived home, my father died. We had spent countless breakfasts talking and resolving any issues we had had in the past. We were so close and to have him gone now just seemed like a cruel joke. I could not help my brothers pick out his casket. I could not help them decide on music. If I had done any of that I would have to accept that he was gone. I recognized the pain from when my grandmother had passed.

My mother knew my entire family was devastated by the loss of our patriarch. My father, Pops to everyone but me, was always the glue that held us together. To ease the sadness after the funeral service, she offered to take all the grandchildren to the miniature golf park for the rest of the day. It was her way of showing my father that she could carry on and take care of the family. She was letting him know she could hold us all together.

Riley stayed for another six months before he returned to Virginia. He would go back to live with the couple he had shared a house with before he left. He was unhappy with his social life in California while living with me. He wanted to go back to free flowing booze and sex. I was happy to put him on a train headed east.

We communicated often. Riley also kept in touch with the kids. But, for the most part, Riley was living the life he wanted.

ONE FLEW OVER
THE COCKOO'S NEST

My life was flourishing. I had a job I loved and that provided me a writing outlet through the newsletters and brochures for which I was responsible. I was dating after more than 20 years. I was attending social events and family functions. I went from one great job just to be hired away by another great corporation. I was deep in the throes of the corporate environment. I was happy. I was at peace. And I was in love, even though I didn't recognize it at the time. I didn't trust anyone and certainly did not -- would not -- trust the concept of loving another person unconditionally. It was so much easier to play the field and not really commit to any man.

Long before the discovery of the "New World" people believed you could sail out on the ocean and then if the ship went too far they would be doomed to drop off the edge of the world.

It was a lot like that. I was sailing along enjoying the breeze and crisp ocean air when suddenly I fell from the edge. If I had been on drugs, I would say that I came down hard from a very high high. I've never done drugs, but I can imagine it would be like that.

I was having a bad day. My spreadsheets weren't coming together. I had a horrible headache and was far more emotional than I had ever been. I don't cry in the workplace. I don't yell or scream or make a fuss. I use logic and reason to get my point across and I write lots of memos. There was no memo written for what I was about to do.

It was as though I was outside of myself. I was watching as I climbed on top of my desk and yelled at the top of my lungs. "What the fuck is going on here???" I knew I was upset that the CEO was buying a new SUV while the file clerks would not be getting a raise. I knew I was upset over the imbalance of monetary distribution that failed to promote the more administrative divisions of the corporation. As I climbed down from the desk – the sound of my own yelling seemed to awaken me to the fact that my behavior was inappropriate. I quickly gathered my things and left the office.

No one had responded to me. No one asked if I was OK. They all just watched as I exited the floor, the elevator and finally the building. I called out as sick the next morning. Still no one questioned my actions.

One thing led to another. I was so very depressed that ending my life seemed like the only answer. I didn't want to die. I just wanted everything around me to stop. I needed to catch up. I needed to just take a second to rest. And I was in physical pain. I ended up in a mental health facility and stayed there for a month. I didn't feel mentally ill. When I looked around at the other members of my ward, I didn't see the connection between me and any other patient.

I told the nurses and doctors that I was in pain. They would give me a Tylenol. When I told them the Tylenol did not resolve the issue, they had a physician come in and examine me. He found nothing and a decision was made that I was simply attempting to get narcotics. I asked for help with relaxation techniques thinking the pain must just be imaginary. But nothing worked. I knew if I ever wanted to get out of there, I needed to stop mentioning or complaining about what I was now considering to be menstrual cramps multiplied by 200. I shut up and was released.

I KNOW ME
BETTER THAN YOU DO

I never in my wildest dreams ever imagined I would be disabled. I had worked since I was 14 years old. Work was personal to me – it was part of my persona. But there the fact was in front of me. I was now on California State Disability and had filed for Social Security Disability. I felt that my life would never be really productive again.

My pain was getting worse and my periods were getting very heavy. After a few months I couldn't leave the house when my periods began and they were coming every two weeks now. I told my gynecologist that I thought I might need a hysterectomy. He hadn't found any evidence that I needed anything that extreme and so I was to start a round of testing. There were multiple ultrasounds, blood work, psychological testing. It seemed never ending and I was getting weaker and weaker.

By the time the doctor concurred that I may need a hysterectomy, I was too weak to have any surgery. I was started on an iron regimen for my anemia. I used cast iron cookware and ate a lot of leafy green vegetables. I drank V-8 juice every day and made sure I ate three meals. It took almost three months for me to gain enough strength to go forward with the surgery.

"Mrs. Riley? Can you hear me Mrs. Riley? We're all done with your surgery and everything is fine." I could hear the nurses, but I could not respond with anything more than a "huh?" I was settled into a room and shortly after my doctor was sitting next to my bed.

Dr. S took my hand and said "I just want to apologize to you personally. I had no idea how truly sick you were." What, this can't be right? He's telling me he's sorry he did not listen to me?

"Once inside, we found your uterus to be filled with pre-cancerous tumors. There were far more than I have seen in a very long time. Also, we had to take the ovaries because they were so encrusted with cysts that we could not save them." He continued, "You must have been in far more pain that I ever thought. I just wanted to tell you I'm sorry I didn't listen to you when you first came to me."

I really didn't care that he was sorry. I didn't care that he didn't listen to me. All I cared about now was getting well. I wanted to heal up and get back to my life. I didn't know what kind of life that would be, but I knew it had to be better than the one I currently had.

Two years later, I was ready to resume some sort of professional life. Emotionally, I was still on shaky ground, but I believed I had the worst behind me and I could move on.

LET'S STOP MEETING THIS WAY

My mother wasn't doing so well. She seemed to be on an emotional see-saw and she was never very clear about her health status. I decided to move in with her and just make sure things were going to be OK. It benefited both of us. Neither of us had to be alone. It was a good plan.

What was not in this plan was my little brother, Charlie, having a massive heart attack and dying before his 50th birthday. My baby brother, the one Mom would not let me touch, the one who had a heart as big as Alaska and reveled in having children around him. He was gone. He left seven devoted children in anguish over his death. My mother was inconsolable and when I tried to comfort her, she told me to get out of her house. I did as she asked but returned several days later just before the memorial service.

Riley called my mother often and talked to her for long periods of time. I don't really know what they talked about, but he seemed to be able to calm her and I was grateful for that. Riley had also been making phone calls to my older brother, Richard. I wondered if they were plotting something. I really hoped they weren't trying to get us back together because I wasn't about to buy any more tickets for that roller coaster.

I was working again. I took a job that I thought would be easy – as a typist for a title insurance company. It turned out to be the start of a new career for me and was far more difficult than I had planned. But, I am an over-achiever who loves a challenge. How could I possibly not love the job?

When I arrived home from work one day, I discovered Richard was there and was planning on staying for dinner. It was finally revealed to me that Riley was returning to California and was going to become Richard's roommate. They wanted to reassure me that this was in no way any pressure on me. They understood and respected my separation from Riley and would not push me to try to make amends to resume my marriage.

Having Riley back in town would not be such a bad thing. He would have his brother and the kids and Richard. He wouldn't need me to hold his hand or give him aid. This was actually a pretty good plan. He could help Richard with his expenses and the two got along just fine.

A couple of weeks after the big reveal of the Richard/Riley roommate plan, my mother called me on my cell phone. The fact that she called my cell phone was very significant because she had always refused to call anything other than a "real" phone in the past. She told me she thought she needed to go to the hospital. This also was cause for concern because she would never voluntarily go to a medical facility without an appointment.

I was in the middle of getting new tires for my car and as soon as the rubber hit the pavement, I was off to take Mom to the hospital. They wasted no time getting her into a bed and something in the back of my brain told me "She's really got something wrong." I watched the heart monitor display and it seemed erratic. There was no rhythm to the lines. All my brothers were unavailable since they didn't all have cell phones. But, I put my sister-in-law in charge of making sure they all knew where our mother was.

She was admitted to the cardiac intensive care unit and plans were being made for her to have a triple by-pass. As they rolled her down the hall to the surgical suite, I gave her a kiss and told her I loved her. I'd see her in the recovery room. She said she loved me too and she'd see me later. A few hours later, my mother was dead. The surgery was a success, but the patient died.

When they came out to the waiting room, Richard was sitting next to me. They started to say they were sorry but... I jumped up and grabbed Richard. *"NO!!! NO!!! Richard!!! Go tell them!! Tell them NO!!"* I collapsed as my big brother wrapped his arms around me. He held me close and smoothed my hair. Several family members went to the phone bank and starting making calls.

That old familiar feeling was back – Grandma, Dad, Charlie and now only six months later – Mom. I hated this feeling. *Helpless. Hopeless. Alone. Longing for a different ending.* But, it wasn't just me. The entire family was thrown into a state of grief. It was doubled in intensity since we had just put Charlie to rest. The wounds were still raw. The question was asked over and over again – how much more could this family endure without breaking?

Riley was informed and he took the news very hard. He had, for some reason, a special bond with my mother. Richard talked to him. He would be there soon. He just had a few loose ends he had to tie up before leaving.

Richard hadn't been feeling so well. He didn't have insurance and his physical condition had been suffering for quite some time. When he did manage to go to the doctor's he was given a diagnosis of several different simple things that could be easily resolved. But, he never seemed to get much better. I suggested that I go with him to the doctor's and maybe I could make them understand that he really was feeling bad.

The plan worked. For once I had a plan that actually worked. Richard wasn't communicating how things were feeling inside his body. He gave the doctor vague descriptions like "It just doesn't feel right." I gave them descriptions as to what I saw and what he said to me. "He feels like his insides are trying to get out of his skin and be his outsides." I explained about the loss of energy. I reiterated every single detail I could remember. Richard was very surprised at the end result. He was admitted to the hospital to undergo some testing.

Two months after my mother's death, Richard was diagnosed with leukemia. His six children rallied around him. But, he needed more than they could give. He needed a way to meet his expenses and he could no longer do that. I put my mother's house on the market and moved into Richard's house. The only problem was that Riley was due to arrive in just a few days and there would be no where for him to sleep.

Alea found a small cottage for Riley that was near her house. He was very happy to have a place of his own and moved right in straight from the train station.

Richard was moved to UC Davis Medical Center. I was his bone marrow match and he needed to get healthy enough to be able to accept a transplant. But, he wasn't doing so well on getting better.

While Richard was in Davis, Riley's landlords told Alea that Riley would have to move out of the cottage. He was too drunk to have on the property. He was often passed out in the drive way after falling down. He left the burners on the stove and the cleanliness inside the cottage was unsanitary. Alea tried to negotiate, but the decision was final – move him out voluntarily or they would evict him. Alea said he would be out in a couple of weeks. He had 30 days, but Alea knew Riley was not safe and she had to do some fancy footwork to find a place for him.

Alea came to me and asked if I could find a place for Riley at Richard's house temporarily. I already had Richard's son and a close family friend in the house. But, I might be able to work it out. I reluctantly agreed to have him stay with me. Alea told me her father had no place else to go. She had tried getting him another place, but she lived in a very small community and everyone knew about Riley's "eviction." No one wanted to rent to him.

Linda Bartee Doyne (aka Linda Jane Riley)

PART FIVE

LETTING GO

During several conversations with Richard after his diagnosis, he asked me to promise to pull the plug if he got to the place where he could not be at all independent. He didn't want to slowly die in some hospital bed while hooked up to tubes, wires and electronic equipment. He just wanted it all to be over.

I reluctantly agreed knowing full well that if that time came, I would not be courageous enough to end his life. It would really not be my decision. It would be up to his children. I knew I would encourage them to let him go, but I couldn't be the one to actually make it happen. So – I lied to Richard and told him, of course, I would do as he asked.

The hospital called and informed us that Richard had a stroke in the middle of the night. They didn't want us to be shocked when we came to visit so they were giving us a heads up.

I walked into his room and the sight was truly frightening. There was a maze of equipment around him. As I walked toward his bed, I could see he was crying. I took his hand and tried to make some kind of light hearted comment. But, nothing was coming out. Nothing was working. He just looked up at me with those pleading eyes. His speech was nearly non-comprehensible. I could make out a few words here and there, but nothing made any sense.

In my heart I knew what he wanted. I knew he wanted me to just reach over and turn everything off. I knew he wanted to just go now. He would rather be dead than to be alive like he was. I put my hand on his cheek and quietly said, "I'm so sorry. I just can't." He jerked his head away from my hand and I could clearly understand "Fuck you! Fuck you!" Those words were the last ones my big brother ever said to me. Each time I entered the room he became agitated and would yell "Fuck you!"

It didn't take Richard long to give up his fight against leukemia. He died just six months after Mom. This was getting to be a six month thing in our family. We wouldn't recover from one death before being faced with another.

I don't care how much you know someone is going to die, the actual death is always devastating. I wanted to help his children, but there was no consolation. I was numb. It seemed I couldn't feel anything. The enormity of the situation seemed beyond understanding. And I felt guilty that I was relieved that he would not suffer any longer. The only thing I could do was to try to keep myself and everyone's environment in good order.

ALL IN THE FAMILY

Riley had been trying to locate his ex-wife, Laura. He had heard that she was in a homeless shelter in our town. When her marriage to her second husband fell apart, it seemed that she fell apart as well. She was an alcoholic and a drug addict. Riley's two older boys had tried to help her many times and each time she would leave their homes and end up in a shelter somewhere.

There weren't that many shelters for women in our town and it took Riley almost no time at all to find her. They had lunch together. I gathered up some clothes and personal hygiene things for him to take to her. And when she was admitted into the hospital, he visited with her. I offered my hand to her in friendship. She was the mother of Riley's two older boys and I felt it was in everyone's best interest to keep things open and friendly.

As a couple, Riley and Laura would have been a jumbled mess of booze and drugs. They would have fed off each other's addictions. In my opinion, their divorce slowed down their personal progression into insanity. I thought it was good that they each had ended up with a person who didn't partake of their substance abuse.

But, what I learned was that Laura's husband had been physically abusive to both her and the boys. I had almost forgotten – until I was reminded – that there was a time when the boys were removed from their mother's home and put into foster care. Riley had been contacted to find out if he could provide a suitable home for them. He discussed it with Lucy and decided not to make any attempts to get custody. By the time I found out about it, Riley had made the decision and there was no changing his mind. I would have loved having those boys with us and making them a part of our family. In hindsight, I should have been stronger, more forceful. I should have taken matters into my own hands.

I don't remember how we got the news about Grant, Riley's second son. All I remember is that I was in shock over the entire situation.

Grant had been a bit troubled in his young life. Who wouldn't be?? He had a non-existent father, an abusive step-father, and a drunk, druggie mother. I had always regretted that I had not pushed for more visitations or more interaction between Riley and his other two boys. But, during that time frame, I was still a pretty meek follower. I was young and thought my husband was smarter, more informed, more rational than I. I believed him when he told me that his ex-wife asked him not to interfere in the boys' lives and let them bond with their new step-father.

Grant had issues with drugs and alcohol when he was a very young man. I don't know what turned him around, but something did. He gave up the life of insanity and took a different road. He was sober and advocated publicly about his new-and-improved life in the world of sane behavior. I didn't know him. I had never met him. But, I was still very proud of his success. It was not my place to be proud, but inside I was smiling.

How ironic is it that his demise should happen as it did? Grant and his wife were very happy. They were expecting a baby in just a couple of months. They already had a boy and they were ecstatic that their family was growing. They frequented many family events and on their way to one such event, a drunk driver crossed the grassy median and hit Grant's car head-on. Grant, his wife and the unborn baby were killed instantly. Alcohol had taken his life – not as anyone would have expected – but its cold hand had reached out and snatched him up anyway. It was beyond sad. It was tragic.

We attended his funeral. I thought Riley would be devastated and I stayed close by his side. But, there were no tears. It was so unlike my family where people openly wept, hugged and did not let go. Riley was reserved, composed and showed no signs of wanting to hug anyone. I saw handshakes, smiles and the words "I'm sorry." But nothing more.

It was a beautiful service and I got a glimpse of Grant's son – Riley's first grandchild. But, Riley just wanted to get out of there and have lunch with his brother and sister-in-law. He had no interest in communicating with his oldest son and definitely did not want to meet his grandson. He did talk to Laura. They hugged briefly. Then we left.

Laura went downhill quickly. Losing a child can be devastating and if you're already prone to substance abuse, it's a quick and easy slide down that slope. This time, her slip ended with her paying the ultimate price. Laura died just a short time after Grant. We attended one more funeral in the same church, with the same attendees, as we did at Grant's funeral.

Laura and Riley had been married seven years and lived together for only four years. Yet, he will tell you he "buried his wife". As far as I knew, I was his wife and I was still alive and kicking. His statement irritated me because I felt it invalidated all aspects of our marriage. Oh well... insane things get said in the world of insanity.

CHANGE OF SCENERY

I was extremely dismayed that Richard's boys were not the little ones that I had once been able to direct. They were now grown men with ideas and lifestyles of their own choosing. I could not stop them from any self-destruction and I could not reason with them to change. I knew my limits. The fact was that it so pained me to be with them during this self-destruction, added to the pain of losing so many other people, I had to get out of that house. No matter how much I tried to clean things up or make things safe, Richard's house was a toxic environment for me and for Riley.

Riley's state of mind was so juvenile at this point that he demanded care much the same as a 12-year old child. He didn't need constant supervision, but he could not be left alone to make unsafe decisions. I had to deal with Riley's growing inability to deal with real life. I took him to our family doctor who asked him if he wanted to try to get sober. Of course, Riley declined his efforts.

Dr. A was honest and open. He informed us that he actually knew very little about alcoholism and addiction. What he did know was that Riley was very close to death and needed to get into the hospital. Again, Riley refused treatment.

Alea, Riley and I left the doctor's office and took Riley back home. We left him there so we could discuss our frustration while enjoying a Riley-free lunch. We decided the best thing was for me to find us a different place to live and get us settled before we did anything more about him.

The Crawford House was a small tract home build in the late 1940s. The garage had been turned into a bedroom with a connecting half-bath. It had a big back yard and was within walking distance to public transportation, shopping and my office. We settled in and made the place comfortable.

Several months later, Alea's husband, John's grandmother died and he went off to North Carolina to attend the services. He learned he would inherit a sizable amount of money and bought a house before he returned home. It wasn't what Alea had expected. But, they had been trying to save enough to buy a house in California for years without much progress. At that time the houses were so expensive, they feared their dream would never materialize.

Apprehensively, Alea requested a work transfer to the Outer Banks of North Carolina and they began making arrangements for the cross-country move. It was several months from departure and I was already missing them to the core of my being.

ADVENTURE IN DETOX LAND

Alea was concerned about leaving her father in the condition that he was in and we decided to make one more attempt at getting him into the hospital. We devised a plan. We told Riley that we weren't sure that he was making his choices with a clear mind. We asked him to detox but that he didn't have to go to rehab. We just wanted him to sign some papers while we knew he completely understood what he was signing. When he agreed we wasted no time getting him to the Center for Recovery which had a detox facility.

During the intake he vacillated between staying and going. But, in the end, we walked with him over to the medical wing and helped him get settled into his room. We told him we loved him and that we looked forward to having the real Riley back in our lives. We were then asked to leave.

The next day, we brought a bag lunch for each of us and planned to have it in Riley's room. He didn't want any of his favorite things we had brought for him. He was having stomach issues and just wanted saltines and chicken noodle soup. He was shaky, but otherwise he seemed to be doing OK. Things were exactly the same when we saw him at dinnertime. Alea and I thought that this wasn't going to be so bad after all. We were extremely hopeful for Riley's future.

On the third day, things changed drastically. We were told that we would not be able to visit him because he was just too sick and to come back the next day.

Day four had me going to the hospital without Alea. I was allowed a visit with Riley, but what I saw shocked me. He was sweating and mumbling. He made no sense and just seemed to be wasting away. The doctor entered the room while I was there. He asked for me and Alea to meet with him later that afternoon. I called Alea and she came as soon as she was able to get away from work.

The doctor informed us that Riley's chances for a full recovery were bleak. He explained that Riley may never be the same if he survives the detox process.

Confused, we reiterated that we had been told that Riley would be hospitalized for a few days while the alcohol cleared his system. We had not been told it would be dangerous or life threatening. We didn't understand why the doctor would be telling us this information now.

Dr B explained that Riley's lab work showed very little liver function and high levels of ammonia. He was an extreme case and they could not have known that until now. In fact, they had no idea how bad Riley was until that morning.

Thinking this must be the worst case scenario, we asked what we could expect if Riley made it through this process. His answer was just as shocking. He informed us that Riley could have been in a black out for an undetermined amount of time. He might not remember why he was in the hospital or even why he was in California. He may not know that we had been separated for years or even recognize his daughter as an adult.

I remember the look on Alea's face. She dropped into a chair as if the news was more than her body could handle. But, she looked up and asked "What else do we need to know?"

"Riley could have extensive brain damage. He may no longer have the mind of an adult, but rather that of a child. Simple things may seem impossible to him – like tying his shoes or brushing his teeth." And then he hit us with the all-time slammer – he could go into a coma and never regain consciousness. There was no medical directive and because of that, there was a possibility that he may be in a vegetative state until we could get all the legalities straightened out. It wasn't enough that I was his wife or Alea was his daughter – we would have to get a court order to give us permission to end Riley's life.

We met up at the Crawford House and picked at the food that my niece, Alexis, had so loving prepared for us. We didn't speak, but there were a lot of sighs. We didn't know what to say. Each of us felt we had put the final nail in Riley's coffin. We paced. We thought. Alea finally broke the silence.

"Why didn't they tell us all this before we admitted him? Why weren't we told of the possible complications?" Her silence, hurt, despair, and guilt had turned into anger. I agreed but said little. I let her vent.

The next day I went to Riley. He didn't know who I was and talked freely about the ogre he that was once his wife. He said how happy he was that whoever he imagined me to be was with him. Shortly after that, he called me "Mother" and said he had done as she asked. He told her he didn't want to go to piano lessons. Only I knew the significance of that statement, but I let it go. Whoever he thought I was, I played along. I wiped his brow and held his hand. I watched the nurses tend to his IVs and medications. I prayed that he would survive.

Alea came to visit that evening and he thought she was me. He was cruel and accusatory. He yelled and screamed. Finally, she left just to be able to keep him calm. When she was gone, he asked why Alea wasn't there.

That night he slipped into a coma. He stayed in that dark place and we didn't know if he would ever regain consciousness.

I got a phone call on the seventh day. Riley had regained consciousness and we could see him. I walked into his room and found him sitting up in bed eating a hearty breakfast. He was smiling, laughing, and teasing the nurses. His hands were still shaking and he was obviously very weak, but he was alert and still in this world.

I was amazed how quickly he had gone from "not here" to being "in the moment." I went from planning his memorial service to celebrating his sobriety in less than 48 hours! Riley knew who I was. He knew where he was. No black out. No brain damage that we could tell so far. He was back.

Riley stayed in the detox center another two days and then announced that he was not planning on returning home. He had decided to enter the center's rehab program and return to the world of sobriety. Both Alea and I were ecstatic! Alea would have her father back and I could get on with my life as a single person. Surely Riley would be getting his own place and having his own life. My future looked bright!

The next month, Alea, John and Ryan left for North Carolina to start their new lives. Alea left knowing her father was going to have a new life as well. My heart was breaking, but I knew things would be better for them. As I stood in the street watching them drive off, I was crying tears of sorrow with a sense of joyful anticipation for them.

LET THERE BE PEACE

Life with Riley was easy for a while because he was not living in my house. The rehab program was three months long and after that he decided to move into a clean and sober house. He stayed there for another four months. Then he came home to the Crawford House.

It had been difficult for me to keep up with the expenses while Riley was achieving his sobriety. I had budgeted for the Crawford House based on having Riley's income combined with my own. Alexis moved in to help with the expenses, but still, it was difficult.

When he decided he wanted to move back in, I could see things getting easier. Riley was always an excellent roommate for his other housemates. I thought he would be a good one for me too. After all, I had seen him at his worst and I still cared about him.

It really didn't make much difference where Riley was living. He went to a minimum of three AA meetings a day and attended every AA social event imaginable. I went to a few with him, but was always met with hostility. To this day, I don't know what that was about, but I ignored it. I was Riley's roommate – not really his wife. I didn't need their acceptance.

WHAT WAS I THINKING?

The lease was just about up for Crawford House and the owners decided to put the house up on the market. I hated the idea of moving, but Riley assured me he would continue in roommate status even in a new house. Alexis agreed to pay more rent and that combined with a raise I had gotten meant we could afford a much larger, nicer home.

I do think that at this time I must have been living on a blue cloud of peacefulness. That cloud prevented me from being realistic and rational about finances and the future.

We found a house that met everyone's criteria which was just tad bit over the amount I had budgeted for rent. I thought – what the hell – I'll take a second job. I wanted that house. One of the most magnetic features was that it had a full size swimming pool perfect for laps and lounging around. It had a backyard that provided complete privacy, so there were many times, I could swim without the encumbrance of a bathing suit.

About four months into the lease, I noticed that Riley was never around. He came by long enough to shower and sometimes sleep, but other than that, he was non-existent. Alexis was around a lot, but the evenings were for partying with her friends. She was young, free and beautiful. It was only right for her to live a full life.

The housing market was slowing down. Things weren't moving as quickly as they had in the past. Professionally, work was slow. My company was starting a series of consolidations. The staff was reduced considerably. I was starting to worry about being employed. I started looking for another job, but the story was the same throughout the title insurance industry. No one was hiring. Houses were just not being sold.

At about the same time, Riley came to me and told me that he wanted to move out. He felt he needed to be living with other recovering alcoholics in order to maintain his own sobriety. He said he would continue to help with the expenses by paying some of the utility bills. A month later he moved into a house with two recovering alcoholics. I wished him well.

Brian decided he wanted to come for a visit, so Riley's room became a guest room for Brian. I was so happy to have him, the idea that I needed a paying body in there escaped me. Brian stayed with me for a month.

Right after Brian left, I was trying to find another roommate for that empty room when I was told that losing my job was imminent. I had not been officially laid off, but I had it on good sources that the staff would be, once again, cut by one-third. I stepped up my job search.

Linda Bartee Doyne (aka Linda Jane Riley)

PART SIX

IF I CAN MAKE IT THERE

One of my potential employment scenarios included a trip to the Los Angeles area. I had been told that if I wanted to stay in title insurance then I needed to relocate to southern California which was the title insurance capitol of the world. If I couldn't find a job in title there, I wouldn't be hired anywhere.

I lined up three days' worth of interviews – mostly with branches of my current company. I had been corresponding with a gentleman on line and we decided to meet while I was there. His name was Duncan and after talking on the phone daily for more than a month, he offered to set everything up. I gave him the locations of my interviews and he found a hotel that was convenient to all of them. He met me at the airport and gave me the keys to his car. He would use his truck while I was there. It seemed he had thought of everything. There were even flowers waiting for me in my room. He took me to dinner and left me at my room without pressuring me for anything more.

My interviews were a hit and I departed SoCal with a job offer. Back at the office, things were proceeding for the layoff. On my bosses desk was an envelope with my name on it. I entered prepared to give my letter of resignation.

"Wait," she said. "If that is what I think it is, hold onto it, because it would be better if you let me give you this envelope instead." I didn't see what difference it made, but took her envelope. It contained my termination papers and a nice severance check. If I had resigned, she wouldn't have given me her envelope and I'd be out the check and any possibility for collecting unemployment. I was thankful for her foresight.

Alexis found two people to move into the house with her. Riley was going to continue to pay for the utilities. I felt I was leaving the Pool House in as good a position as I could. The remaining tenants agreed to let me use the garage to store my belongings for six months.

Three days before I was to head down south, I got a phone call to tell me there had been a change. A current employee would be taking the job that had been promised to me. Since we had not signed any contracts, they were perfectly within their rights to hire someone else. My plans were falling apart. I called Duncan and commiserated over the ill fortune.

A SMALL DETOUR

I am a Certified Professional Secretary and worked in administration management before getting sick. It was time for me to expand my search options. I started putting out resumes as an executive or senior administrative assistant. But, I had been out of the arena for so long, my credentials didn't seem valid.

A friend was the Executive Vice President of a manufacturing company in St. Louis. He called and offered me a job with such a decent salary. It was an offer I could not refuse. I would only move my essential items.

The thought of just getting into a relationship with Duncan and then moving half-way across the country was extremely uncomfortable for me. He was the first man I really felt positive about in years and I was not even giving it a chance to get started. I knew I could care deeply for him if I gave it a chance. But, there wasn't time. He assured me we would continue via internet and phone calls with occasional trips to see each other. I knew he meant it, but I also knew that long distance relationships are nearly impossible to maintain.

My time in St. Louis was miserable. The job sucked. My friend was not too great of a vice president and the owner of the company was his girlfriend. The company seemed to be on the edge of disaster with too many strong personalities and too much paranoia. And, although I was making better money, I was drowning in debt from trying to help out with the Pool House and getting caught up from my employment limbo. To top it off, I was trying to get a new place to live and I had no furniture or anything to stock it with. I was truly starting over even though the job was only a six-month commitment. Duncan and I had not managed even one visit and the internet/phone dates were slowing in frequency. At five months, I gave notice.

FROM WORSE TO EVEN WORSER

Back to the job hunt drawing board and back to SoCal. I was once again promised a job with a branch of my previous company. But the day after I arrived, I discovered the entire department had been dismantled and there were no jobs to be had. Duncan didn't know I was back in town and I wasn't going to call him for help. I made do. I spent a week in a cheap motel where there was a murder in the courtyard. I spend one night in my car. It was one of the worst times of my life. Although, I had a temp job, I was homeless and broke.

I don't remember how I connected with Kenny and Joannie, but they saved my life. They had a room for rent and the same night I interviewed was the night I moved in. They quickly became my family and I adopted not just the couple, but the entire family. I had found a job with a title company that specialized in foreclosed homes. After about a year, I knew it was time for me to leave, but their house would always be one of my homes.

My interaction with Riley was minimal at that time. I had heard that he was drinking again, but still attending AA. In fact he was the district representative for his group. I found that interesting and confusing. It was more of Riley pushing the envelope to see how far he could go with unacceptable behavior before anyone stopped him.

When I moved into the house in Upland, Carrot came to stay for a while. But, she couldn't handle the scorching hot summer air and missed her children almost unbearably. She returned to the SF Bay Area where she was far more comfortable and happy. I missed her terribly.

Duncan was in and out of my life like a yo-yo. We would spend months of seeing each other often and then we would slip into months of nothingness. When we were together, it was like we had never been apart. When we were apart it was love at a distance without expectations. After all, I was still, technically, a married woman. And, as it turned out, Duncan was still, technically, a married man. Neither of our marriages had any effect on our relationship. We knew we loved each other, but we were lazy and didn't put each other as a very high priority. I suppose I should have worked harder at keeping us together. Then, again, he should have worked harder at keeping me around.

It was while I was living in Upland that I got that awful phone call from Brian's fiancé. While I was working, loving Duncan and enjoying my time alone in my cute little bungalow – my son was dying. So now, I needed to get my head out of my self-absorbed sand and get back to the business of taking care of myself and my family.

NO I DID NOT!

I had just come back from the ladies room and picking up a bottle of water. It seemed like it was taking forever for me to get back to my desk. I could see it, but I just didn't seem to be able to get to it. Finally I was there, I sat in the chair and tried to remain focused. I picked up a file and laid it in front of me, turning each page slowly but not seeing any of the words. Everything in my eyesight had a slight haze around the edges and there were black spots in the middle of my vision.

I thought I had called out "Rey?" But Rey, my supervisor, was busy trying to explain some legality to one of the other examiners. "I don't feel so good." I laid my head on my desk. Just then Rey turned around and saw me. "Are you OK?" I remember looking up at him and in my mind I was screaming – NOOOO! I was not OK. I knew I was going to pass out.

The ambulance came and took me to an emergency room. One of the other examiners was by my side and I was grateful she was not planning on leaving anytime soon. Then I was off to get tests done and blood taken -- poked and prodded. A heart attack was suspected and I was admitted.

I didn't believe it. Even after a week in the hospital. I just could not believe that I had had a heart attack. There was no excruciating pain. My left arm did not even tingle. I simply felt as though I was going to faint. That's it. I did NOT have a heart attack because those are not the symptoms of a heart attack.

The doctors showed me the lab results, EKG's, and they talked and explained. OK. So... maybe... I had a heart attack. I was released and went home to an empty house. Alea could not come out. There was no one to help me. Ryan was about to go out on summer break and it was decided he would come out to California and help me recover. I'd gladly accept that I had a heart attack if it meant that I would have my grandson with me for a while.

This young man of 18 was very good to me. He drove me to my appointments, cooked my meals, drew me a bath, and just made sure I was well taken care of. OH… there were issues. After all, he was only 18. He found plenty of time to party with new found friends from the neighborhood. I didn't care. He was there for me.

The cardiologist made a determination that my attack was partially caused by stress and ordered me not to return to the office environment. However, I managed to convince him to let me work from home. Since my work was all internet based, I was able to work off my home computer. My human resources department helped me become the first ever telecommuter in the history of the company. If all things went well for me, they would have others working from home as well. I was determined to make this work.

With my office set up and my routine established, I was able to successfully complete all my files in a timely manner. It was appearing that the work-from-home project was turning out to be successful.

At the end of spring break, Ryan returned home. His stay only reinforced my need to be closer to my family. The only way I could make that happen was if I cut my expenses to the bone. I called Kenny and Joannie and asked if one of their small cottages would be available for rent. They had several properties out in the desert area and I was hoping that one was coming available. When they said yes, I jumped at the chance which cut my rent by more than half. Now I could save some money for the move.

INTERVENTION

Right after Ryan left to go home, I received a phone call from a friend of Riley's – one of his girlfriends. I liked this particular woman and thought that she was actually someone who could be trusted. She was a recovering alcoholic who had a logical head about her. But, she was married, which, ironically, made her just Riley's type.

She seemed a little frantic when telling me what was happening with Riley. She said I needed to come down there right away because there was about to be an intervention to get Riley into detox and rehab.

What?? I wondered who these people were that thought they could succeed where his entire family had failed. They didn't know his history. They didn't know about his last near-fatal detox. I knew that each time an alcoholic goes through detox it is more dangerous than the last. It's possible that Riley might not survive another detox. We had just lost Brian, this family could not go through this again so soon. I asked her to see if she could find out more details and who I needed to call to put a stop to this.

It was too late. The intervention was planned for that night. A group of Riley's AA friends were gathering at his house and would make an attempt to get him into the center. In my mind, I thought, these are smart people. They know forced rehab just doesn't work. Why are they doing this?

Riley went back to the Center for Recovery and was admitted into their detox ward. I decided I would not drop everything and go up there. His girlfriend was there and she agreed to keep me informed.

I expected this to not end very well. I expected that Riley would be dead within the week.

Things started happening exactly as I had expected. The phone calls from the medical people at the center informing me that Riley would not make it were a source of anger for me. I was angry at the interventionists. I was angry with Riley for agreeing to go. I was angry that we would be forced through this one more time. The girlfriend called me three times a day with reports on his progress.

I relayed the information on to Alea who was displaying very little emotion. Within the past few months, her brother had died, her mother had a heart attack and now her father was dying – again. I knew there was emotion in there, but I also knew she was numb.

The seventh day into the detox process, when Riley was coming out of the danger point, I got a call from the girlfriend informing me that she had been barred from visiting Riley. The doctors were refusing to give her updates or any information at all. I called the center and got the same brush off. I finally got through to a floor nurse who told me that Riley said that after the way the girlfriend and I had treated him, he wanted us to be out of his business.

I knew that he had no recollection of what had transpired and any "wrong doing" on our part was simply in his imagination. It could have been something that happened years ago or never have happened at all. I told the girlfriend there was nothing more either of us could do. I didn't have a power of attorney and legally had no rights.

Riley got out of detox and stopped at the liquor store on his way home. So much for interventions.

Linda Bartee Doyne (aka Linda Jane Riley)

PART SEVEN

A DANGEROUS MAN

The caller ID said "Riley" so I answered with a cheerful "Hey you!" But it was not Riley, it was his roommate Bob. I liked him. He had been Riley's roommate for many years and it seemed Riley had a good thing going with both Bob and the other roommate, Steve. Bob was a lawyer and circuit court judge.

"I just wanted to tell you that I'm having Riley committed as being a danger to himself and others. I wanted to give you an opportunity to come get him if you didn't want him committed."

Riley was not a part of my life. Why would I care what happens to him? My response was for Bob to do what he felt he must do. I thought that would be the end of it. I had hardened since the last detox when he accused me of doing things that were never clear to me about what they were. I was trying to just not have anything to do with him.

"Mom, can you meet me at Dad's? I'm coming to get him to keep him from being committed." The voice on the phone was Alea. I couldn't believe Bob had called her. I needed to keep this from happening. Alea had a good life and adding Riley to the equation was a recipe for disaster. She had a two bedroom/one bathroom home that she shared with her husband and son, son's wife and brand new baby girl. Where would she put a drunk without much potty training? No. I would not allow her to take on my responsibility.

Duncan called that week. I told him that I had stayed married in order to keep my military benefits. He already knew that. And I knew that someday I might have to "take care" of Riley. It was time for me to pay the piper. We talked about how my moving to North

Carolina and having Riley living with me in the tiny cottage would mean we would probably not see each other again. Our timing had always been so off kilter. Maybe someday… but we knew it was over.

A few weeks later, I rented a truck and car dolly, loaded them with Riley's belongings and made the trip. He looked atrocious with his skin almost iridescent green and his eyes covered by a film of yellow. He had scrapes, cuts and sores up and down his arms and legs. He couldn't walk without holding onto something and he stunk. It would be a long drive.

I didn't want to drive through the night. I stopped at a motel so we could start out fresh in the morning. I managed to get Riley a bottle of vodka and some mixer. I also got us some food from a nearby restaurant. When I returned to the room, he was not there.

Frantic, I raced around the motel complex looking for him. I had just about given up when I saw him with another traveler. The man was guiding him back towards me. "That's my wife." Riley was saying. "It's OK. We found her. See she's OK," responded the good Samaritan.

Evidently, Riley thought I had been gone too long and so he went out to find me. He wandered around the motel and then entered this gentleman's room saying he was looking for his wife. Riley had no idea where he was or why we were there. All he knew was that I was not in that room with him.

I wanted to throw out the bottle I had just bought and get him to the hospital ASAP. But, I decided to let him have his way. Let him have his drunk. Once I got him home, I'd try to get him some help. Besides, Dr. A had told us a long time ago that when an alcoholic is in as deep as Riley, taking away the booze could be very dangerous.

DISCOVERY

Once we were home and settled in, I started doing some research. What I really wanted to know was how long someone in his condition could stay alive. I looked up cirrhosis and followed the links to several websites. I only knew of that one complication, so that's where I started. I spent an entire weekend just looking up everything I could about alcoholism, cirrhosis and all the other complications I discovered in the search. I started a check list of the symptoms I saw in him just during those few days together. The pages that follow covers the conditions, symptoms, etc., that my research uncovered.

CIRRHOSIS

Because this is the best known alcohol related disease, I decided this would be the best place to start my research.

With the consumption of large quantities of alcohol, the liver becomes scarred and the scar tissue blocks the flow of blood through the portal vein. The portal vein carries blood from the intestines to the liver. The more scar tissue created the less the blood the liver can process. The liver is a "blood cleaner" tool. If the liver doesn't function properly, the affect will be more toxins, such as plasma ammonia, not being eliminated. The blood will begin to thin and contain more toxins which in turn creates the increased risk of infection.

Some of the signs and symptoms of a malfunctioning liver include:

Jaundice -- yellowing of the skin and eyes

Fatigue and weakness

Loss of appetite, nausea

Red spider-like blood vessels visible just under the skin

Swelling of extremities, i.e., hands, legs, feet from fluid build-up

Swelling of the belly

As the liver damage increases other diseases develop. The liver is a miraculous organ because it can regenerate some potions of itself if the alcoholic ceases ingesting alcohol permanently. However, the scarring will remain and each time alcohol consumption resumes the less time is required for additional scarring to begin. By the time cirrhosis has been diagnosed, other complications have developed that are not as forgiving as the liver.

I read the words that seemed to repeat as I went from Wikipedia, NIH, WebMD and other websites. It may have all been worded differently, but the meaning was the same.

It appeared to me that Riley had all the symptoms of cirrhosis. That wasn't surprising to me since the color of his skin was a big give-away. But this must be just the tip of the iceberg maybe he was exhibiting signs of some of those other complications that the websites talked about. I continued my research. Alcoholic pancreatitis seemed to come up at each site, so I plugged it into my search engine.

ALCOHOLIC PANCREATITIS

The pancreas is a small organ with three purposes: 1) provide digestive enzymes; 2) provide insulin and glucagon hormones; and, 3) secrete large amounts of sodium bicarbonate. The three functions all aid in the digestion of food, regulating sugar levels and neutralize acid in the stomach.

Pancreatitis is an inflammation of the pancreas. The metabolism of the alcohol in the pancreas is similar to the function of the liver. The metabolic process creates by-products when, in excessive amounts, accumulate in the ducts and create a blockage. If the blockage continues, the enzymes begin to digest the cells of the pancreas. The pancreas becomes inflamed and ceases to function.

Symptoms of alcohol induced pancreatitis can include:

> Yellowing of the eyes
>
> Back pain
>
> Nausea and vomiting
>
> Fever
>
> Diarrhea
>
> Lack of appetite

I didn't know about the pancreas. Oh, I knew we all had one, but I didn't know its real function or why it was important to have one. This was an interesting bit of news because it seems Riley fit all those symptoms as well. What else didn't I know? I clicked on one of the links in an article.

HEPATIC ENCEPHALOPATHY

With the liver not functioning properly, the plasma ammonia levels raise and are transported to the brain via the bloodstream. The ammonia makes a home in the frontal lobe of the brain and interferes with brain's function.

Some symptoms of hepatic encephalopathy may include:

Lack of awareness (Is not aware of actions taking place around him)

Inverted sleep pattern (Sleeping all day and staying awake all night)

Irritability (Everything is a source of irritation – mostly imagined)

Tremors (Uncontrollable trembling or shaking movements)

Somnolence (A strong desire for sleep or sleeping for prolonged periods of time)

Asterixis (Uncontrollable movements of the arms and wrists)

Ascites (Accumulation of fluid in the peritoneal cavity)

Disorientation (Confusion as to place, time, people)

Amnesia (Inability to remember day to day or even longer)

Uninhibited behavior (Ignoring personal hygiene, use of foul language in the presence of children, anything society would deem inappropriate)

Seizures, Coma and Death (eventually, if untreated)

Whether or not the damage is permanent depends on how long the alcoholic has been abusing. Some of the symptoms will disappear during the detox process, but some may never go away. The ability to remember is sometimes greatly hampered even when sobriety has been attained, leaving the alcoholic with dementia.

This disease is graded as to the severity based on the West Haven Criteria.

Grade 1 – Trivial lack of awareness

Shortened attention span

Euphoria or anxiety

Grade 2 – Lethargy or apathy

Minimal disorientation

Subtle personality change

Inappropriate behavior

Grade 3 – Somnolence to semi-stupor, responsive to verbal stimuli

Confusion

Gross disorientation, bizarre   behavior

Grade 4 – Coma (unresponsive to verbal stimuli)

I guess there is no grade for DEAD.

Hepatic Encephalopathy leads to or is somehow connect to Wernicke-Korsakoff Syndrome. My research wasn't clear if it was just another name or if it was a side complication.

WERNICKE-KORSAKOFF SYNDROME

This is a condition resulting from a thiamine (Vitamin B1) deficiency. When alcoholics stop eating balanced meals, they lose valuable vitamins and minerals necessary for the body to function properly.

The symptoms may include:

Confusion;

Tremors;

Changes in vision;

Loss of short-term and long-term memories;

Hallucinations;

Muscle weakness and atrophy;

Lack of coordination;

Appearance of poor nutrition.

Well, there we go again. Here was another thing I didn't know and that was starring me right in the face. The

more research I did, the more I was in awe that Riley was still walking around on this earth. I was exhausted. I had been at this for more than two days. But... just one more click for tonight. I wanted to know more about a term that had been used when Riley was in a previous detox. I had a vague idea, but I wanted details.

Linda Bartee Doyne (aka Linda Jane Riley)

DELIRIUM TREMENS

Latin for "shaking frenzy", Delirium Tremens (DTs) are also known as "the shakes". DTs occur upon the cessation of alcohol consumption after a long period of habitual drinking in large quantities. The condition carries a 5% mortality rate with treatment and 35% without treatment.

Symptoms usually don't occur until between the second and tenth day of alcohol withdrawal. They include:

Tremors of the extremities

Confusion

Diarrhea

Insomnia

Disorientation

Agitation

Hallucinations

Anxiety

High pulse, blood pressure and breathing rate

Treatment includes the use of medication such as benzodiazepines, such as Valium, Ativan or Librium. Additional drugs are used to control the hallucinations.

It is never advisable for an alcoholic to go it "cold turkey" without any medical assistance. It may seem brave, but bravery is often met with death.

I understood now. I could now see why Dr. A had told us not to stop giving Riley alcohol. It seemed counter-productive at the time. I often felt I was just leading him down a path ending at his grave. But, Dr. A would not have told me to keep buying it if it wasn't necessary. Oh, sure he explained it all, but I didn't really understand until now.

I found all these things from reading Wikipedia, WebMd, eMedicine, and the National Institute of Health websites. The more I searched the more I found. I read so much that my eyes couldn't focus. It was time to find a doctor and get some help.

So far, I knew he definitely had cirrhosis, probably had Type C and Grade 2 Hepatic Encephalopathy, Somnolence and Ascites and maybe even Alcoholic Pancreatitis. I believed I had enough information to provide to the doctor, but first I had to find one.

ENTER DR. H, ADDICTIONOLOGIST

It took a lot of patience and even more research. I called general practitioners and family medicine doctors. Most would not treat alcoholics who were still actively drinking. Others had no experience dealing with alcoholism. Many offered to help get him into detox and rehab. My frustration level was rising rapidly. I called the local AA service center and had no luck getting a referral from anyone. I called local rehab centers, but those doctors only treated patients of their center while they were in house. Then I stumbled upon another website for a rehab center out in the valley. The difference was that their medical director had a private practice in town.

Dr. H was an addictionologist which means he is a medical doctor specializing in addictions. I thought a doctor of this sort would be able to give me answers to hard questions. I had no hope of Riley going into rehab and attempting recovery once again.

In spite of how a person gets into a health situation, they still deserve an attentive medical professional who can – at the very least – make the end less painful. That was what I wanted for Riley. If the end was near, I didn't want him to suffer. And I needed to know how close we were to the end.

Memories of Brian floating off to heaven while in a coma ran through my mind. I was hopeful that the same departure was in store for Riley.

However, Dr. H was more interested in what he could gain in the form of professional accomplishment of "curing" an alcoholic who had been drinking for 40+ years rather than monitoring his health. In fairness to Dr. H, his goal was to get people into rehab and saving the alcoholic's life, not watching them deteriorate. I think he truly believed that Riley could be saved. I sometimes thought he was just as much in denial as Riley.

Dr. H told Riley he was greatly shortening his life expectancy by continuing to be a practicing alcoholic, but that he could be his "poster child" for the possibility of recovery. I thought, OK, if that worked it would be great, but I wasn't going to hold my breath.

I related all the things I had discovered and asked if Dr. H thought Riley had any of the complications that I had researched. He nodded and said the lab test will show the whole story. He handed me the lab work order and I saw that the potential primary diagnosis was hepatic encephalopathy and secondary was pancreatitis. Hummmm…. That spoke volumes.

Dr. H prescribed a daily dose of Lactulose to help counter some of the ammonia in his frontal lobe. The super sweet liquid would also help with the anger that seemed to overtake Riley on a moment's notice. He was also prescribed a variety of vitamins and minerals as well as Campral, a drug to help reduce the cravings for alcohol.

The lab work came back and I was given a copy of the results for my records. I didn't know what I was supposed to do with it, so I shoved it in my purse to be filed in Riley's medical file. I had no clue what those numbers meant. It was all just goggle-lee-gook to me.

In spite of all this, Riley continued in a downward spiral even with the medications. It became obvious pretty quickly that Riley would not be anyone's poster child for anything except an advertisement for Aristocrat Vodka.

EXPIRATION DATE

Dr. H turned over Riley's medical monitoring to Dr. G who was an associate in his practice and an internal medicine specialist. Dr. G was helpful in monitoring and providing insight into Riley's health. I found him to be an excellent doctor who was as open as he could be without making predictions.

The one thing that was the most disturbing to me was that I kept asking Dr. G how much longer he thought Riley would be around. His response was always the same.

"No one can tell how long each of us has. Only God can make that determination." I could not get Dr. G to state that Riley was in fact dying and therefore could not get him to anticipate how long Riley had left.

It was frustrating for me. I didn't understand how a doctor could tell a cancer patient that he has X amount of time, but no one could give me an estimate on Riley. I felt that Dr. G may have been fearful that I might bring a law suit against him and that was why he was guarded in his wording. Instead of stating the Riley was dying – he referred me to grief support groups and set me up with hospice care.

Dr. G told Riley that a person's body cannot withstand or survive the effects of alcohol in large quantities for a very long period of time. But did not say… "Riley you're dying and if you don't stop you will be dead in less than six months." It was what Riley needed to hear, but it never happened.

A friend told me about an alcoholic who had a liver transplant. It seemed odd to me that an alcoholic could get a new liver when the first one was abused so badly. But the idea was interesting and maybe I could find some new information by doing some more research.

LIVER TRANSPLANT

Riley once told me he had a plan. The plan was to drink for as long as he could – until he was near death. Then he would detox, stop drinking for six months and apply to UNOS for a new liver. After the transplant he would resume his trip down Alcoholism Lane. I think he's in for a rude awakening because I discovered that only 14% of all transplantable livers go to alcoholics.

Approximately 95% of alcoholics with cirrhosis never receive referrals for a transplant because they cannot stop drinking long enough to even begin the process of meeting the requirements. UNOS (United Network of Organ Sharing) has strict guidelines for alcoholics needing a new liver as a result of cirrhosis. They must:

Abstain from alcohol for a minimum of 6 months;

Completion of a substance abuse program;

Weekly attendance at Alcoholics Anonymous meetings;

Successfully passing a psychological examination;

Regular comprehensive physical examinations.

Once on the list, if any of the requirements are not met or if the alcoholic slips, they are permanently removed from the list. I could see Riley completing most of the requirements, but he would never be able to pass the psychological exam. Those psychologists are trained to decipher fact from fiction. Riley was not that good of a liar.

While I was reading about transplantation, I learned how people were prioritized on the UNOS list. There was a formula used to determine life expectancy without a new liver. The ones with the shortest time left were closer to the top. My analytical mind told me that if the formula could be used to find out who would die first, maybe it would work on alcoholics. The issue was still the same – a degeneration of the liver.

There were two formulas – the MELD Score and Child-Pugh Score. I found information on Wikipedia.

HOW LONG HAVE I GOT, DOC?

MELD SCORE

If a person with a failing liver is fortunate enough to manage to get on the UNOS list for transplantation, the person is evaluated for the chance of survival without the transplant.

Typically the determination is made by assigning a MELD (Model for End-Stage Liver Disease) Score which is a number calculated by using information obtained from three segments of a blood test. The resulting score will determine the severity of the disease and predicts the chance of survival over the next three months. Liver transplant patients are placed on the waiting list based on who has the shortest life expectancy without the transplant. The MELD Score is used, along with other factors, in making that determination.

When the doctor orders a blood test, he will include in the order a Comprehensive Metabolic Panel along with Prothrombin Time (PT) with whatever else he is ordering. These tests will provide the information you need for determining the MELD Score.

There are three segments of the blood test needed to calculate a MELD Score:

INR or PT – International Normalized Ratio for Prothrombin time – Measures the ability of blood coagulation (clotting). The reference range is usually around 11-16 seconds; the normal range is 0.8-1.2. In a person with cirrhosis the blood will take longer to clot than a person with a healthy liver. If you don't see "INR" on the test results, look for "PT" (Prothrombin Time).

Total Bilirubin – excreted in bile and urine, is responsible for the yellow color of jaundice, bruises and urine. Look for "Bilirubin, Total" on the test results. It should be with the Comprehensive Metabolic Panel section if several tests are on the same report.

Serum Creatinine – Measurement used to determine renal (kidney) function. If patient had dialysis at least twice in the past week, this score will be 4.0. Look for "Creatinine, Serum" in the Comprehensive Metabolic Panel results.

Along with the information that was necessary was an explanation of how to calculate the score.

By entering the values of the tests in the chart below, and adding the values together the result would be the score:

Test	Value	
What is the INR?		
What is the bilirubin? (TBIL)		(mg/dl)
What is the serum creatinine?		(mg/dl)
Has the patient had dialysis at least twice in the past week?		
MELD Score: (Total of result values)		

40 or more   =   71.3% mortality rate

30-39   =   52.6% mortality rate

20-29   =   19.6% mortality rate

10-19   =   6.0% mortality rate

9 or less   =   1.9% mortality rate

If the alcoholic has a score of 40 or more it means that he has a 71% chance of dying in the next three months. If 30-39, a 52.6% chance of dying in the next three months… and so on…

CHILD-PUGH SCORE

This score is also used in determining the possible life expectancy of a person with liver disease. However, it uses two additional factors and estimates the prognosis of survival for one or two years. Points are given for each measurement, the points are then added up to get the prognosis result. The two additional factors are ASCITES and HEPATIC ENCEPHALOPATHY. Before I could continue, I needed to find out what Ascites was.

ASCITES

Ever notice that your alcoholic's tummy is starting to look like a "baby bump"? It could be the start of ascites which is a swelling in the stomach area due to an accumulation of fluid in the peritoneal cavity. It can also manifest with swelling in the ankles and legs (peripheral oedema). There are three classifications or grades:

Grade 1 =   Mild, only visible on ultrasound and CT

Grade 2 =   Detectable with flank bulging

Grade 3 =   Directly visible

SCORING:

To calculate the Child-Pugh Score, use information from the lab reports to determine which point level is appropriate according to the following chart:

Function	1 point	2 points	3 points
Total bilirubin	Less than 34	34-50	More than 50
Serum albumin	Less than 35	28-35	More than 35
PT INR	Less than 1.7	1.71-2.20	More than 2.20
Ascites	Grade 1	Grade 2	Grade 3
Hepatic Encephalopathy	None	Grade 1 & 2	Grade 3 & 4

Add the points to determine which class level is appropriate for your alcoholic:

Class	Total points from scoring chart	One year survival	Two year survival
A	5-6	100%	85%
B	7-9	81%	57%
C	10-15	45%	35%

A **Class A** score means there is a 100% chance of survival for one year and an 85% chance of survival for two years.

A **Class B** score means there is an 81% chance of survival for one year and an 57% chance of survival for two years.

A **Class C** score means there is a 45% chance of survival for one year and a 35% chance of survival for two years.

Since the doctors were unwilling to estimate or guesstimate Riley's logical life expectancy, I decided to use these two methods to find out for myself.

I rummaged through my purse and pulled out the results from Riley's blood test. Then I entered the information into the charts. Riley had 71% chance of dying within three months according to the MELD Score. He was a Class C in the Child-Pugh Score which meant he only had a 35% chance of surviving another two years. Either way, the results were not good. But, I was satisfied. I knew now what to expect. I just wished I could get a medical professional to confirm my discovery.

THE END IS NEAR

I was thankful for the visiting nurse and the home aides. They were able to get Riley to do things that I could not get him to do – like take a shower. I imagine that having a woman helping him wash his body must have been delightful for him. It was definitely delightful for me because I got relief from the smell of rancid sweat. Also, the nurses were extremely honest and open. They were the ones who told me Riley was within six months of death. One told me six months was a very optimistic estimate. She predicted a few weeks rather than months.

A few days later, Riley was displaying signs of internal bleeding by having coffee-ground like feces and vomiting blood. I urged him to let me take him to the emergency room. But, he did not want to go. The nurse and aide both explained how important it was for him to go to the hospital. He was adamant – no hospital.

There is this little trigger in our human brain that is set off by "the right thing to do." I firmly believe everyone has this trigger – even the most abhorrent murderers probably have it. They may choose to ignore the signal generated by the trigger – but I think it is still there.

I can't ignore my trigger. I tried to ignore that noise in my head telling me – "Get him to the hospital!"

"Linda, in all likelihood, if Riley goes to the hospital, he is going to die there. His body is so weak that I doubt he will make it through the detox process." She hesitated and then said "There is another option, but I don't know how you will feel about it and I don't want to offend you." Her words were slow and low and I knew she was about to say something that needed to be kept off the record.

"I have not called Dr. G yet for orders. I'm not even supposed to be here today. This isn't my regular day, but you live just up the street and I thought I'd just see how you were doing. No one knows I'm here – yet. I am scheduled to visit Riley on Monday." I was trying to follow what she was saying.

"You could wait until Monday and then I would call Dr. G. You can see how Riley does over the weekend." She took my hand and asked, "Do you understand what I'm saying to you?"

I nodded my head and thanked her for the information. She gave me her home number and told me to call her if I managed to get Riley into the hospital. I thanked her and before retuning inside the house and watching Riley wipe the blood from his nose and mouth – I took a walk around the block. I didn't think another ten minutes would matter one way or the other.

My stomach was doing flip flops and my brain was spinning. I was not the love of Riley's life and really didn't think I should be the one to make this decision. But, I would not burden Alea and I knew Riley's brother would not comprehend the severity of the situation. If I understood the nurse correctly, Riley wouldn't last through the weekend. Then again, he probably wouldn't last even if he were admitted.

Everything moral inside me said "Save him. Do everything you can to save his life." But, what kind of life would it be? More of the same? More attempts at him completing his goal of drinking himself to death? Wouldn't it be more humane to just let him go? What was I thinking? He's not a dog, he's a human being with a life – such as it is. I'm not God, I'm just a caretaker with no right to prevent him from living as long as his heart will beat. Well, it's not really up to me, is it? Riley has made it clear that he does not want detox or rehab. He wants to drink until he dies. I felt this moral dilemma was weighing heavily on my soul, my heart and my brain.

I returned to the cottage and found Riley sitting in his chair with his puke waste can between his legs. His nose was bleeding and he was still vomiting blood. I couldn't stand it any longer. The "preserve human life at all costs" side of me kicked in and I called 911. They had been to our place many times before.

It was a small space and I backed out of the way when they came in with all their equipment. "Hey there Riley! What's going on today? Are you ready to go get some help?" They joked around with him trying to get to him accept help through their playful bantering. Finally, they took me aside and asked me if there was anything I could do to convince him to go to the ER? I knew what I had to do – I had to manipulate him to do what was necessary.

I told Riley that if he didn't go to the hospital, I would stay on his back every single hour of every single day until he agreed to go. I told him I would take away his Vodka and not allow him to drink while he was in my house. Riley made no objections to being admitted.

The ER doctors took me aside and told me to expect the worst for Riley. They did not give me any hope at all that he would survive. He needed surgery to repair the esophageal and stomach bleeders. He would probably not make it through the surgery, but if they didn't do the surgery, he would slowly and painfully bleed to death. I told them to proceed with the surgery and then I waited. I was thankful that I had gotten Riley to sign a medical power of attorney right after he got to SoCal.

I didn't know what an esophageal varices was and I knew I had to look that one up in my Wikipedia as soon as I got home.

ESOPHAGEAL VARICES

The definition of esophageal varices occurs when the scarring on the liver prevents blood from flowing through the liver sending that blood flow through the veins in the esophagus. The lining of the esophagus is irritated by the alcohol as it travels down the throat and into the stomach. The alcohol is caustic and wears away the mucus membrane. The blood vessels become thin and the walls weaken. The pressure from the extra blood flow causes the esophagus to balloon outward and rupture. When the rupture occurs, the bleeding may be extremely rapid and death can be imminent.

There are no warning symptoms for this condition unless there is a bleeding "drip" rather than a rupture. That is the bleeding may be only a small tear in the esophagus. In this case there may be symptoms of:

Black, tarry, "coffee-ground", and/or bloody stools;

Light-headedness;

Paleness;

Vomiting and/or vomiting of blood

Since alcohol is a blood thinning agent, any tiny tear or lesion can become a life-threatening situation. Alcoholics have been known to bleed into their stomachs and eventually bleed to death before anyone would notice.

Riley was comatose. The surgery went well, but his chance of regaining consciousness was unlikely. It was just a matter of time. As I waited for the inevitable, I thought back... how many times had I been told he was going to die? How many times had he gone into detox and the doctors would emerge from his room with predictions of imminent death? I tried to count... 4, no maybe 5 times, in the past three years? I wondered if he had nine lives like a cat, or if he had finally reached the end of his luck.

I thought back to the previous tears shed by my children as they believed their father was about to leave them forever. Memories of vaguely planned memorial services and calling our pastor kept creeping into my brain. And then... the miracle that he survived and the elation of the kids when they realized they could possibly end up with a healthy, sober father. It was always followed by the disappointment of watching him crawl back into the bottle and resume his drunken lifestyle – which did not include them. They were always left with anger and pain – so I hesitated calling Alea this time. I would wait.

OH... YOU'RE ALIVE

Riley opened his eyes and slowly came back to life. He was incoherent. The hallucinations were full bore and the tremors prevented him from having any control over his body. He could not feed himself because he could not control his hands. He had no strength to even lift the fork to his mouth. He did not know why he was in the hospital or even who I was. Slowly he recovered... he did not die... instead he was discharged and admitted to a nursing home where he could regain his physical strength. He was in the nursing home for six weeks.

I couldn't help but think to myself – "Is this guy immortal or what?" One more time he had been pulled back from the brink of death. Dr. G told me he would not have lived if I had not taken the action that I did. Riley should be grateful he has people in his life who have kept him from dying.

Riley was not grateful. Instead, he managed to get to the store and buy a bottle of vodka. It had been less than a week since his discharge from the nursing home. He was back on his track of self-destruction. In less than a month he was back to drinking almost a half-gallon a day.

Since Riley was no longer within six months of death, he was no longer eligible for hospice care. All the outside help disappeared. I was on my own.

I pushed to move us across country to North Carolina where my daughter and grandson lived. They would be able to help me with Riley and I would have some occasional relief from the insanity.

I made a presentation to my manager about having me take the work-from-home project to the next level. I wanted to move to North Carolina and still work for the office in Irvine, CA.

It took about a week to get all the necessary approvals and details squared away. We made the move within just a few weeks and set up housekeeping in a house in the Outer Banks. We fell into a routine. It wasn't a routine that I liked, but Alea and Ryan were there to help and because of that, things were a bit easier – at least for a while.

Linda Bartee Doyne (aka Linda Jane Riley)

PART EIGHT

THE HART HOUSE

Our house in the Outer Banks was up on a hill. The driveway was so steep that some cars just couldn't even make it. It was a huge two-story home with a large kitchen and lots of space. We converted the formal dining room into a bedroom for Riley. There was a near-by half-bath that we designated as his. The view from his room was of the sound and was the most beautiful view in the house.

The household consisted of me and Riley, Ryan and his pregnant wife (Nicole) and their 3-year-old daughter (Emily), and also a friend of Ryan's (Justin). I loved having so many people in the house. Everyone enjoyed my home cooking almost as much as I enjoyed cooking for them. I also loved having people around who were actually capable of having conversations. For a while, life was good in the Hart House.

Ryan had adopted a Chesapeake Retriever/Australian Shepherd and named her Jade. She was a feisty puppy and hadn't settled down much as she grew towards becoming an adult. He asked me if we could take Jade on as our own. Riley had been asking for a Bull Mastiff and although Jade was much smaller, maybe Riley would like her. Jade joined our family in the big house on the hill.

Jax had been my cat from when I lived San Bernardino County before Riley ever came to stay with me. He was a spoiled king of the house and was willing to let all know his status. I worried Jade and Jax would not get along, but I was wrong. In no time at all they were playing and chasing as though they were both the same gender and species. Everyone was fitting in just fine.

A typical day for Riley would begin with morning conversations that were all relatively sane. We would discuss what we will have for dinner and what needs to be done around the house. I always ask him what he is going to do with his day. He never has an answer. I ask if he wants to start a grocery list – he always does.

During our morning chats, he runs to the bathroom several times. Sometimes he returns with wet streaks down his pant legs where he has missed the toilet. Sometimes the seat of his pants will be soiled where he has not wiped the feces from his butt. He then sits back down at the table and wants to resume the conversation. When he transfers himself to the living room, I will wipe down the dining chair and the top of the table with a bleach wipe. I have covered all the cushioned chairs with towels which I remove and launder in extremely hot bleached water.

With a fresh drink in his hand, and once in the living room, Riley turns the TV to NCIS, House or Law and Order. Sometimes he'll watch Burn Notice or some other similar show. This is where he sits nodding in and out of sleep for several hours. Every time he wakes up from nodding off, he comes back to the kitchen for another drink. At this point conversations with him have degenerated to him making demands and complaining about what he perceives to be inadequacies caused by my caretaking. I won't let him drive. I won't let him live alone. I won't let him have a credit card.

When he feels the need for a nap, he will stand and balance his footing, then takes a step towards the fireplace mantel. He follows along the edge of the mantel to the TV cabinet then to the door frame and over to the bookshelf just inside his room. He finally reaches the edge of the bed where he falls onto the mattress. He removes his clothes from the waist down and settles in for a snooze. Jade will snuggle up to him and the two will be peaceful for a while. These naps usually last a couple of hours.

When he wakes, the bed will be wet from his urine. He uses the desk and door jamb to get to the bathroom then returns to his room to put on the same clothing he had on before he laid down. He makes his way back to the kitchen and fixes another fresh drink. That's when lunch happens.

Riley takes everything out of the refrigerator that he thinks may interest him as food for that day. He takes out anything left over from a previous dinner, all the deli meat, hot dogs, bacon, eggs, etc. He usually decides on a leftover that I've failed to throw out when I would think it was unsafe to eat. He'll warm it up and eat a couple of bites. It then sits on the counter, or in the microwave or in the oven. If I don't check, the plate of food might sit for 2 days. If Riley discovers it, he will resume eating it as though he just fixed it that day.

The afternoon routine continues the same as the morning with him alternating between watching TV, taking naps and sitting at the dining table. The only change is that in the afternoon he is more likely to fall and unable to get himself upright. I can't pick him up because he has no muscle control and I can't lift his weight. He will pass out on the floor, wet his pants and eventually crawl to a chair or his bed.

Sometime around 5 p.m. Riley starts his quest for dinner. Standing next to the table, he will let all in ear-shout know that dinner is to be served by 7 p.m. – not 6:55 or 7:03 – but at 7 p.m. exactly. He will want to know what I plan on cooking and how it will be cooked and do I have enough of everything. He will rant about the dinner issue for a good hour before he tires and takes another nap.

At 7 p.m., when we are all seated at the table for dinner, Riley's plate is prepared and put at his place. He seats himself and dabbles at his food, pushing it around his plate with his fork. A couple of bites make it to his mouth and remnants will stick to his beard and mustache. The rest of the diners remind him to wipe his face. He wipes his face and retreats to his room – with only a couple of bites taken from the dinner that he demanded so vehemently.

It's nap/bedtime. He's done for the day. I cover his plate because he will be up during the night and likes having leftover dinner to pick at when he's awake. In reality, he only takes a bite each time he is up – so I wonder why I fix him dinner at all. Oh yea… now I remember… he has to have his dinner at 7 p.m. or his world will disintegrate.

We lived on the Outer Banks for a year and what had begun as a peaceful family life had digressed in a house filled with frustration and anger. Ryan, Nicole and Justin spent most of their time in their rooms. After dinner they would retreat and that's where they would stay. I didn't blame them. It was impossible to watch television in the living room which was Riley World. If he heard the television on, he would get up and come in making his way to his rocking chair. Once there he would change the channel to whatever he wanted to watch. A three-year old didn't stand a chance of watching SpongeBob.

HAPPY NEW YEAR

Our huge front yard had a fire ring and often Ryan and his friends would gather around for an informal party. I loved hearing the laughter and listening to music that made no sense to me. It was the sound of young people being happy and I was grateful to be able to look without being inside the circle.

I'm highly allergic to smoke, dust, and dirt. During the times of the fire ring gatherings, I would leave the window open for as long as I could, but would always end up sitting in a hot shower and using my inhaler after closing the window.

On New Year's Eve 2009/2010, Ryan and Nicole had a small party around the fire ring. This time the smell of the smoke hit my room and I seemed to lose any ability to breathe. I couldn't catch my breath. When I did, my breathing was labored. I was suddenly frightened. I called Alea and she told me to get into the shower – Now!

I stayed in the shower for what seemed like a very long time. My breathing was easier, but still labored. I exited the bathroom and lay down on my bed. I called Alea again and told her I thought I should go to the hospital. She came over right away. It didn't take her long because she only lived down the street. By the time she entered my room, I was having the worst headache I thought I had ever had. It was splitting my forehead in half and my left eye felt like hot needles were stuck right in the center.

Alea gave me some migraine-strength aspirin and cool washcloths. She sat next to me rubbing my back and smoothing my hair. She talked softly telling me it was going to be alright. I calmed down. I started to breathe normally again and I drifted off to sleep while being happy I did not have to endure spending the night in the emergency room with drunken New Year celebrators.

The next day, I felt twinges of the headache and my eye was still hurting, but it was nothing that I couldn't deal with. It was New Year's Day and Alea and Nicole were in charge of dinner. There was nothing for me to do except hide out in my room and rest. I took advantage of it.

I could hear little crackles in my eye when I rubbed it to try to clear the fuzziness. Many years ago I had had a cataract removed from that eye and an artificial lens had been implanted. My first thought was that somehow that lens had become broken and bits of glass were now in my eye. I made an appointment with an ophthalmologist.

There was no waiting period when making the appointment with the eye doctor. I made it in the morning and I was in his office by the afternoon. I thought – business must be slow.

As he was peering into my eye, the doctor was on his cell phone making a dinner date. I wondered if his love interest knew he was multi-tasking. I also wondered if he was giving me the full attention I needed.

He pushed back and rolled his stool away from me. "You've had a stroke."

"No. I've never had a stroke." I responded. I thought he was asking me if I had ever had one. I didn't realize it was not a question, but a statement.

"Yes you have. It's called a Retinal Emboli and you are now blind in your left eye."

"I can see just fine. I can't be blind."

He then held up a card in front of my right eye. All I could see was white. But, if I simply closed my eye, I could still see with the left. The doctor explained to me that the brain remembers the image and uses it to replace the vision when the right eye is closed. If you block the vision, the brain has nothing to remember.

My next question was how long it would be until my eyesight came back. The answer was never. I would never have sight in that eye again. I offered up solutions because I refused to believe that in the 21st Century there wasn't SOMETHING that could be done. But each solution was not viable.

The eye doc suggested strongly that I either go to the emergency room or to my primary care doctors – immediately. I went home and made an appointment with my cardiologist.

Before I could get to the cardiologists, I ended up in the emergency room anyway. I was violently ill with vomiting and diarrhea so bad that I felt I'd never get out of the bathroom. I thought I must have a really bad flu. Just to get to the ER, I wore double diapers and carried a pail. I couldn't remember when I had ever felt so bad.

The doctor came in and told me he suspected that I had Salmonella. He asked a bunch of questions about where I had eaten in the past week and what had been my activities. He was trying to find out where I had gotten the illness, but I knew exactly why I was sick.

I had cleaned Riley's bathroom which was covered in feces and urine. I wore gloves, but was barefooted and did not wear a mask or goggles. I must have contracted the germs from there. The doctor agreed, but since I had eaten at a local restaurant that would have to be checked out.

I went home and locked myself in my room so I would not expose anyone else to the horribly uncomfortable illness. I went downstairs only when I knew that Riley was the only one in the house.

The ER doctor has explained to me that I will always have susceptibility towards stomach infections and that I must be very careful with hand washing and other personal hygiene matters. He explained how to clean Riley's area without exposing myself to further harm.

So I finally made it to the cardiologist. It was only semi-good news. It appeared I may have had a second heart attack about the time as the stroke. He confirmed what the ophthalmologist had told me and that I would not be seeing with my left eye ever again. The good news was that I knew what I needed to do to prevent a second stroke, third heart attack and Salmonella. I was to take better care of myself. That was it. That's all there was. This was only the second week of the New Year and I hoped this was not an example of what was to come.

Linda Bartee Doyne (aka Linda Jane Riley)

HOW CAN I GET SOBER?

"New Beginnings" is a substance abuse help center serving the local area. Ryan and Nicole were discussing it as an option for one of Ryan's friends. Riley got in on the tail end of the conversation and thought they were talking about him. He was adamant that I should take him right away to talk to the counselors at the center. He had questions and knows they can help him live in sobriety.

"I want them to tell me how I can maintain sobriety and still drink my vodka."

Stunned... we all looked at each other and someone said... "Isn't that called an oxymoron?" Riley was looking at us... waiting for a confirmation that he had finally found a way to make everyone happy. He was too fuzzy to recognize the comment about the oxymoron. Someone replied that one of us would be happy to take him to the center and find out what if they could answer his question.

Riley left the room and we all just kinda gazed at each other as we sat around the table. It was Ryan who made the first sound... "Uhhh... well... awwrighty then..." We all broke out in laughter. There really wasn't much to say, we just enjoyed the moment of comic relief.

I made the appointment. Bless her heart, she tried – and she tried some more – to make sense of what he was asking. By my barometer, she was young – no more than 35 which is young to someone who is 60. But, she was also experienced and educated. You could tell she had dealt with some hard and fast addicts in her job. She knew her stuff.

The counselor suggested that he get sober and then find his own answer to his question. He insisted that he didn't want to stop drinking, he just wanted to know how to stay sober. He didn't want to detox because detoxing was not fun. He didn't want to go to rehab and he didn't want anything to do with AA. He just wanted to be sober and keep drinking.

As the appointment came to a close, I realized that she never told him he could not be sober and still drink. She never told him he could either. What she said was that maybe, if he wanted to gradually cut back on his consumption, he could be more sober than he was currently without going to detox or rehab. But, she stressed that he would have to want it more than anything he had ever wanted in his entire life. She wished him luck and said he was welcome to return whenever he wanted to talk. As we were walking to the door, she said to me, in a low voice, "You have your hands full with this one. Come in if you need some support." I nodded in the affirmative.

Someone asked me if it is possible for an alcoholic to gain sobriety without going to an in-house rehab center. My answer is… for someone who is not end-stage that is possible if they have the determination and a strong support system. If they do not need medical detox, they can achieve sobriety. But the odds are not in their favor. Long-term sobriety is most often attained by committing to a treatment center that offers care even after the alcoholic has graduated back into society. The longer the in-house stay, the more likely the alcoholic will stay sober. So the answer is yes, but not likely. And the rehab center must provide a solid program for the family of the alcoholic. Everyone needs to heal.

I think we non-alcoholics sometimes forget how strong the pull is between the bottle and the alcoholic. Have you ever seen one of those giant magnets that are attached to the boom of a crane and used to pick up cars? Image a safety pin as the alcoholic and the magnet as the booze. There is no contest the magnet will win every time. That safety pin will have to have help to free itself of the magnet. The help is detox and rehab centers, a strong family support system and support program.

HOW OLD ARE YOU?

It was a Saturday morning in August and I was working on the budgeting at my computer when Emily came down from her room. She typically would get up before her parents and I would fix her some breakfast. It was our special time together.

Riley was watching television in the living room – or so I thought. Emily would walk through the living room and say good morning to Riley as she passed by. But this day, I heard her come down the stairs and then just stop before entering the living room. I got up to see what was stopping her. Riley was standing in the living room with his penis in hand. He was urinating right in front of the television set. Emily was staring at him with her little mouth open. She didn't know what to do. I rushed over, picked her up and took her to the kitchen.

I was shaking. I was angry. I was in disbelief. Tears were streaming down my face. I hugged Emily tight and held on. She was confused and quietly said "MeeMaw, too tight." I let go and asked if she would like some waffles. Of course she would – it was one of her favorites.

It appeared that I was more traumatized by the experience than Emily. She was just confused and disgusted. I was devastated that a grown man would do something like that. I hadn't realized until now how bad things really were.

I made the decision to move Riley to the country. My thought was that he would have less influence on the youngsters and I would have more control over how his alcoholism affects the rest of the family. I wanted to get him far enough away that he would not be in daily contact, but close enough that they could come for planned visits.

Within the week I had lined up several houses for my inspection. Alea and I started out on our road trip and the minute we walked into Brick House, we knew it was the one. It had a huge office at one end of a long rancher and the bedrooms at the other end. It had a "homey" feeling. It wasn't the giant Hart House, but it was the right size for us.

But, we were to have one more experience with Riley's immortality before the move took place. After suspecting that Riley had had a stroke, Alea and I took him to the emergency room.

It wasn't easy. If he had just wanted to have him be admitted for detox, the hospital would have turned him away. In fact, three other hospitals refused to admit him or treat him in any manner. But, because there were definite indications that he had in fact had a stroke, the hospital that treated him in the ER and was forced to admit him.

It was DejaVu all over again. Everything played out very much the same as the previous hospital scenario. He's not going to make it… oh… I see… you are still alive.

This time when Riley was released, his attending physician advised him not to return home without first getting some physical rehabilitation. We were also told that the extent of the stroke eliminated the possibility of Riley ever living alone again. He would have lapses in his memory and would often seem confused. We couldn't find a nursing home within 200 miles of us that would accept him. He was too much of a risk. So he came home.

GIVE ME THE COUNTRY LIFE

The Brick House sits in the middle of an acre lot. On the left and right there are acre sized horse paddocks. To the rear is a crop field and across the street is another crop field. Our nearest neighbor is across the street. If you extended a line across along our property line the edge of our property would still be about 50 yards to theirs. Other than that, our nearest neighbor is about a quarter mile up the road.

The house was a long, brick rancher. At one time it had a garage but it had long since been converted to another room. It had windows all around which provided a beautiful view of the yard and horse paddock all the way to the tree-lined property perimeter. It was the perfect room for my office with build-in bookshelves and a window seat.

There were three more bedrooms at the other end of the house. Sometimes if felt like a hike to get from one end to the other. The kitchen was a good size but could have used some updating and it opened up to a den with a large fireplace. Off the kitchen there were French doors that led to the formal living and dining rooms. All-in-all it was a lot of space. It was perfect for us.

I grew up in what then was considered the country. I loved living there. As an adult, I prefer the country life over the city. I love not having my neighbors know everything I do by virtue of listening out their back door. I love having a yard that can accommodate a large garden. I love letting the dog out to endless exploration without a leash. I love having the cat leave me a mouse on the front step every morning. I love the smell of the fresh air without exhaust fumes.

And --- I love that Riley can't walk to a liquor store. I love that I have control over when he leaves the property and why. But, even without Riley, I would still love and live in the country.

The closest convenience store has fresh dairy items only on Tuesdays when the truck comes. They usually sell out by Wednesday afternoon. Inside the little store is a pizza shop, but they do not deliver. They are open 7 days a week from 7 to 11.

In the other direction there is a little country store. It isn't so much a convenience store, but truly a country store. To get to the door you must walk up a few steps onto a wooden porch. There are some stands with live plants and even an elevated "cat area" where the owner's cat greets all patrons. When you walk in you half expect there to be a big pot-belly stove in the center with chairs around and peanut husks on the floor. But, sadly, there is not. When you walk into the store you are instantly hit with the smell of country ham. There are big jars of pigs' feet and pickles on the counter. There is also a wooden stand filled with fresh grown seasonal vegetables.

At the back of the store is the most wonderful meat market around. The meat is all fresh cut to order and you can order pre-designed packages at a very reasonable cost. There are also giant wheels of cheddar cheese and cured meats hang on the wall in random order. You won't find any gourmet items here, but you will find local honey and true country type fare. You will also not find any alcohol of any type. Every local resident comes here eventually and the proprietors do their best to remember everyone by their name. It doesn't feel like a step back in time. It feels like down home country goodness.

Both the convenience store and country store are only accessible by automobile. They are not within walking distance. There are only a few businesses that could possibly be reached on foot.

A tire repair shop, the post office and a beauty shop are all about three miles from our house. If I were desperate, I could walk there, but it would be difficult. There are no sidewalks. The roads are flanked by pastures and front yards of country homes. By most people's standards, we are basically isolated.

Riley and I quickly fell into a routine. I get up very early (sometimes as early as 4 AM) and go straight to my office. Riley joins me by bringing me my morning coffee. He sits across from me and we have a brief conversation. Sometimes we talk about things around the house or Jade and Jax or what's going on with my blog. Those conversations are typically enjoyable and provide Riley with some interaction with a human. But on other days... well... it's different.

Riley loves the city. He prefers everything to be in walking distance. He loves having his neighbors so close that you can hear them flush their toilet. He doesn't mind walking the dog on a leash and using a pooper-scooper. He doesn't mind changing the cat's litter box. His idea of a garden is a tomato plant on the balcony. Over his morning coffee, he likes to plan and then shop for tonight's dinner. He loves the urban lifestyle. Most importantly, he would love to take back control over his coming and going.

During one of our morning conversations Riley told me he wants to move back to the city. He states that what he wants more than anything is for ME to live with him in the city. Of course, this gets my attention because for most of the past 40 years – I have never been the woman he would have CHOSEN to be ANYWHERE with. So I pressed him on the issue.

After the long drawn out explanation as to why he wanted to be with ME in the city – the truth came out. Riley knows he can't live alone if he is drinking. He doesn't really want to live with me. BUT – if he lives with me in the city, he knows I'll take care of him as he actively continues his alcohol adventure. I'm not the chosen woman — I'm just the only one left who will take care of him.

"You better get used to overalls and plaid shirts." I told him.

WANNA HEAR A CLEAN JOKE?

I was busy in my office. I didn't usually pay much attention to what was going on in the rest of the house if things were quiet. Riley wasn't drinking, but the stroke had left him with a very short attention span.

I could hear some scuffling about in the kitchen and little innocent barks from Jade. I thought maybe I'd check it out as I poured myself another cup of coffee.

This particular morning, Riley loaded the dishwasher and confused the liquid dish detergent with the dishwasher soap. The result was a kitchen full of soap suds. The suds reached over the top of the toe kick of the counters. Jade and Jax were sliding through the suds and jumping on them. Each jump sent bubbles up into the air and Jax was truly enjoying chasing them around the kitchen. Jax jumped high to catch the floating bubbles, while Jade scooted around the kitchen floor.

It was a sight to behold. Instead of thinking that I was now going to have to stop what I was doing and clean up the mess, I was standing in the middle of the suds watching Jade and Jax as they entertained me. The suds could wait. They would melt down and then I could go in and clean it all up. I would have the cleanest floor in the county!

I looked around and there was no one there but me. Riley was sleeping and I wished he had been awake to share this moment with me. I called Alea, but she was busy and the verbal description was just not as humorous as the visual. I wish I had a video camera so I could have posted it on FaceBook.

A BLOG IS BORN

I woke up one morning and watched an incredible sunrise. The entire sky was turning from yellow-orange to bright blue. I watched in amazement. I was so enthralled that I wanted to share it with the world. Something this beautiful should never be forgotten. I went to the computer and wrote down a description of what I saw. It was just supposed to be a description and that's all. I didn't really intend to do anything with it – except send it to Carrot or Georgia. But that couple of paragraphs ignited something in me.

In my family we have several forms of communication – e-mail, Facebook, telephone and tele-Logan. If you tell one member of the family something, it will quickly spread throughout the entire family. These rapid-fire quips often inspired a family member to call me and ask for the true dirt. Sometimes I was getting four calls in a day. I got tired of repeating the same information over and over again.

During one of these phone calls with Alexis, she said I could make things easier for everyone if I just kept a blog. A blog??? What was a blog?? She patiently explained to her dear old auntie that it was simply a journal that was kept on on-line and accessible to whomever wanted to read it. Oh!! That sounded like a great way to communicate!

I began my blog, The Immortal Alcoholic; on October 19, 2010 I wrote my very first post for my blog. I was so excited because this blog would do more for me than just allow me to communicate with my family. It would give me an outlet for creative writing. It would chronicle my journey with Riley. And who knows – maybe someone will read it and I might find others who are in my very same situation.

A DEADLY COMBO

Since being out here in the country, Riley has been more focused on transportation; primarily on his own transportation. We have countless discussions and arguments ending with Riley having a temper tantrum. His claims that he can drive just as well drunk as he can sober fall on deaf ears. I will not budge on the issue. I will not be a party to putting a drunk on the road.

Over the past two years, even before we moved to the country, I have made sure that Riley could not get behind the wheel of a car. He has a little red Toyota that he wants to drive. It's a constant source of irritation for both of us.

Riley's point of view is that he's been driving drunk for more than 15 years and, therefore, knows how to drive when he is intoxicated. He has never had an accident so he must be doing something right. He has had a few DUI tickets, but nothing more sinister than that.

I must admire the fact that he has thought this out and has used logic to argue his point. It doesn't matter that it's a warped point of view or a point of view that could kill some unsuspecting person. It is his point of view. But my admiration ends there.

It is unconscionable to me that any person would put another person's life in danger in such a manner.

Even though Riley was not currently drinking, I refused to let Riley leave the house on his own. He went with me to do shopping and we even got to go out to dinner. We explored our new hometown and agreed that it was simple and sweet mixed with a lot of history. It had everything we could want. At least it did for me. Riley always preferred the city. If he had his choice he would be back in San Francisco.

Those were "reasonable" times in our life. Riley understood that the stroke made it impossible for him to live on his own. So there was no discussion about him going back to California on his own.

I was still working at my telecommuting title insurance job. It and my blog consumed most of my days and there was little time left for me to focus on Riley. At one point, I was so overwhelmed with work that I couldn't go to the grocery store to get some much needed supplies – like – cat food and toilet paper. I remember this day because it was just about the end of my "reasonable" Riley times.

The road back to insanity was slower than it had been in the past. This time I handed him the car keys and fretted the whole time he was gone. I wasn't very productive while he was gone so I could have just gone myself. But, when he returned he had not been drinking. He did not buy any alcoholic beverages at all. This put me into a false sense of hope.

I continued to let Riley venture out on his own whenever it seemed more time efficient. He must have made those trips to town more than a dozen times.

We had rented a car for the weekend and I needed to return it to the agency. They had a service that provided transportation back to the house after returning the car. We had used this pick-up and delivery service many times.

The day the rental car was due back. I was swamped with work files. Being a telecommuter, I have an obligation to maintain a higher-than-average production level in both quantity and quality. I was on overload because a new job task has been assigned to me and I needed to show that I could handle the fluctuating requirements. If I can't keep up my end of the commitment, I'd be forced to return to the office environment – which means moving 3,000 miles from Alea and Ryan. That was not an option.

Also, I expected the delivery of a sizable quantity of office supplies and the delivery of my daughter's birthday present. My signature was required for the supplies.

All of that meant that getting the rental car back to Enterprise was going to be a problem. Adding another day would be costly. So I made a decision. I decided to delegate the car rental return to Riley. He had been doing so well… surely he could handle this. I was basking in the warmth of the last few months of his sobriety. But history does, in fact, repeat itself.

First off, I must say, Riley did not return home in a drunken state of mind. But, he brought home with him a bottle of his old friend Aristocrat. He didn't hide it. He took it out of the bag and put it on the kitchen counter. It was a smaller bottle – about half the size of the one he used to go through in about a day's time.

He justified his purchase with the fact that it was a "cheap" bottle of vodka. As if it really mattered to me that he could have spent more dollars. The monetary expense was not as important as the sanity expense.

I asked if we could talk about it before he cracked that seal and unleashed a whole lot of craziness. And we did talk. I listened to him tell me that he needed to see if he could handle just taking a drink or two a day. I listened to him explain how he thinks it might be different since he can't get to the liquor store very often. I listened and it was as if I could say the words before they ever came out of his mouth.

Then I asked him to listen. I told him that I would not buy any booze for him. Once he emptied that bottle – I would not make sure that he got replenishments. Whatever the results of drinking that bottle were – would be results that he created. I reminded him that without transportation it would be difficult for me to get him medical attention quickly. I reminded him of further brain damage that could result. I made sure he heard me reiterate all the reasons why he should not take that drink.

Once again, we began driving to the store together. He was still sober enough for me to have him accompany me, but I was not going to allow him to drive. I thought that because he had just returned to drinking that I could at least control how much he was drinking and what he was drinking.

I made a fuss when he put the cases of beer into our cart, but he didn't care. He just made a fuss right back. I succumbed to his demands. Several times, he would disappear while I was shopping. I would be reading an ingredients label or calculating a price when I looked up, he would be gone. I would search the store for him, but he would not be locatable. I often assumed he was in the men's room. He almost always had to make that visit each time we were in the store. I honestly thought that he was still inside the store.

What I didn't realize was that the state liquor store was in the same shopping strip as the grocery store. It was easy for Riley to slip out of the grocery store, visit the liquor store, hide his bottle in the car and then return to the grocery store. The little side trip might take him no more than 15 minutes. I take on average an hour and a half when I do grocery shopping. That 15 minutes wasn't really noticed so much especially when Riley has been known to spend up to a half-hour in the bathroom.

Riley was able to conceal his liquor store excursions for more than a month when I figured it out. I felt so stupid when I found the bottle of vodka under the back seat in the stow-away compartment. I seldom used those compartments except for water bottles and maps.

But on this particular day the compartment wasn't closed completely so I opened it. There it was. It all made sense to me. The reason behind all the disappearances was crystal clear to me now.

I confronted Riley. He was adamant about wanting to continue drinking vodka. In fact, he was going to do me a favor and save me the cost of the beer. He was just making me buy it to make me assume that beer was all he was consuming. I could not believe how insanely rational he seemed. I told him I would not be buying him any more vodka or beer or wine. I informed him that his adventure in seeing how far he could push was over.

Riley still had a supply. It was hidden somewhere in the house – at least I thought it was. He was obviously drunk now. Where I was so busy with everything else, I didn't pay much attention before, now I was on high alert. It was suddenly clear that Riley had crossed that fine line between being drunk and being in the position of not being able to stop without help.

I didn't buy the vodka for a while. But the Listerine was disappearing from my bathroom closet. The vanilla extract was disappearing from my pantry. I needed to decide what was the lesser of the evils.

Riley was adamant about not going to detox or rehab. He was adamant about his choice of death over sobriety. I knew there was only one thing left for me to do. I went to the liquor store and bought him his coveted gallon of vodka. It took less than a day for him to drink half of the bottle.

So now… the roller coaster has begun a new realm of fun and I had, in fact, bought a season ticket. I cried while I was in the liquor store. I cried on the way home. I cried thinking about Alea and Brian. I cried that Riley had been the gift of so many chances and Brian had none. I cried because I was watching someone commit a slow painful form of suicide. I cried as I thought about the day we met. I cried over the fact that his was once a genius of a man who used reason and logic to live his life when he was a very young man. I cried as I remembered all the abusive situations he had created over the years. I cried because all I wanted was for this to come to a final end.

FEMALE COMPANIONSHIP

May 7, 2011 started a whole new round of Riley living in a lovely little state in the country of Riley World. The name of the state is Denial. The residents of this state have no responsibility except to themselves. The only meaningful activity practiced there is imbibing in alcoholic consumption. There are no illnesses, no drunk driving tickets, no consequences of alcohol abuse.

Riley has lived there before and has returned to this place he calls home. This is where he is most comfortable and he believes there are others who feel the same way. I know for a fact that he is not alone in this state. But the problem is that most of the people do not communicate with each other. However, Riley asked my assistance in locating one of the females who might be interested in sharing this state with him.

Personally, as a woman, I see no reason why any woman would be attracted to Riley. His boyish good looks had been replaced by the appearance of a man much older than Riley's 70 years. His skin and eyes were jaundiced, his fingernails were uncut and unclean, his hair was greasy, and his body emitted an odor that almost made me gasp for a breath. He did not and could not drive. Because I wouldn't give him access to a credit card, he had to ask me for cash when he wanted to spend some money. I saw no reason why he would attract someone of the opposite sex.

I asked Riley what he thought he had to offer a potential romantic partner.

Riley was very matter of fact and totally serious when he stated, "I have a big dick, big bank account and a prescription for Levitra." I supposed that in Riley World and the State of Denial, that's all that's required to have a meaningful relationship.

I asked Riley how he thought I might go about finding him a girlfriend. He told me that if I would just let him drive to town he would find one at a bar. I informed him that driving either of our cars was just not an option. However, I would be happy to drive him to a bar and then he could call me when he was ready to come home. Riley didn't like that idea.

I then suggested that I could drive him to the bar and get him a motel room. Then he could call me the next day when he was wanted to come home. That would give him plenty of privacy for his meaningful overnight relationship. He didn't like that idea either.

The next option was to write a personal ad for him to post on a dating website. We could work out the details when he found a suitable match. He liked that idea and went off to write his ad and Google dating websites.

As he was leaving my office, I imagined an ad posting that went something like this:

> *Physically and financially well-endowed senior male seeks much younger woman with big tits for intimate encounters. My interests include vodka guzzling, watching porn, cop show re-runs, the weather and NASA channels. Cleanliness is not a factor. Must be willing to provide transportation. No long-term commitment necessary.*

I just knew his in-box would be packed with responses.

LIFE IS SHORT FOR SOME

The month of May 2011 was not going to be considered the best month of my life. I was tired. It seemed I was always fighting a cold or a stomach bug or something. When I consulted my primary care physician, I was told that I was diabetic. I didn't need medication because I could control it with diet and exercise. I felt that the reason for my feeling under the weather was now explained.

At about the same time I discovered a lump in my neck. I ignored it thinking it was just the result of sleeping with the fan on full force all through the night. I thought the lump was just the sign of an infection that would go away in a few days.

During one of my phone calls to Carrot, I mentioned the almond-sized lump growing under my jawbone. I made light of it, but Carrot was angry. She made me promise to go to the doctor's immediately. I thought she was over-reacting, but I know better than to try to argue with her. She seldom gets angry with me so I paid attention.

I went to see my doctor again and met with his physician's assistant, Erica. She examined the lump in my neck and told me she needed some blood. Then I was asked to wait in the little waiting area until the results were in. After a short time, Erica asked me to join her and the doctor in the examining room.

The doctor re-examined my almond. He put his hands in my mouth and asked me to stick my tongue out and then in and then out. He asked me a few questions and then told Erica to schedule an aspiration. The doctor then left the room.

Erica told me that it looked as though I may have a growth on my lymph node. I knew she was talking about lymphoma. I asked her if she thought it could be anything else. She said there are very few illnesses that present in that manner. Also, looking at my recent complaints of feeling tired and general malaise, all fit in with that condition. Besides, the fact that the almond was hard and not really painful was a real cause for concern. She told me she wanted to be prepared for the worse and expect the best.

I left the office in a bit of a daze. I could be dying. I could be dead before Riley. That would be the ultimate slap in the face. I didn't know if I should tell Alea or wait for the final verdict. I just kind of wandered around. I called Carrot and gave her the news. She told me originally her mother had been diagnosed with lymphoma before she got the lung cancer that killed her. She said I MUST tell Alea.

I consulted Dr. Google and found that the type of lymphoma that I most likely had would usually mean a 70% chance of living more than 5 years. That's not bad – I thought. I can do a lot in 5 years. I'm 62 and that would mean I have an expiration date at 67 years old.

The following Saturday, Alea came out and we went over the money. I told her where it would come from and how I wanted it dispersed. We talked about her taking care of Riley and how to handle that situation. I told her I had a 5-year plan for what I wanted to accomplish and I needed to start right away.

On Wednesday I had a CT scan and got the results the same day. I am "cancer-free". The lump is a severe infection of the submandibular gland – in short I have an infected spit gland. It is treated with antibiotics, rest and drinking lots of water. I was ecstatically happy. I was alone in the car while I made the 2 hour drive towards home. I had a lot of time to think.

How ironic it would have been to have Riley outlive me. One more thing Riley could hold up to the world – "see I told you I would live longer than you – and you didn't drink!" My goal of keeping Riley from living with Alea would have been for nothing because the decision would no longer be under my control. It became very clear to me what I must do.

I would get the diabetes under control and get myself as healthy as humanly possible. I would stick to my five-year plan for my future. Most importantly, I became determined to not take for granted anything that life has to offer.

BIG BROTHER IS WATCHING

When the 2011 season of television programs were presented, I was especially interested in the program "Person of Interest". I thought this show had a really good Orwell-esque concept. It reminded me of the radio program that told George Orwell's story of a society where the government watched everything everyone was doing at every single moment of every single day. It's where the term "Big Brother is Watching" originated.

The premise of the "Person of Interest" story is that everyone around the world is being watched by someone at all times. It may not happen intentionally, but there are videos, recordings, etc. of our daily activities. One of the main characters has invented a machine that informs him when someone is in danger. The other main character takes the information and makes a valiant attempt to prevent whatever the "wrong" from happening. Hummmmm... wouldn't that be a wonderful thing?

I thought the theory was good. The reality might not be so good. I don't think that device has been invented yet, but that's OK because our law enforcement agencies have something else they can use. They have computer geeks who can hack into our computers and see what we look at, what we order on-line, our financial history, essentially, all of our computer activity. I have never had anything to hide. I have never felt too threatened by the fact that a cop somewhere might find out that I'm searching for one of those soup-making blenders. What does concern me is the fact that they have carte blanche to rummage around in my space without any good reason why.

In December 2011, three law enforcement officials came to my door. They wanted to talk to Riley about his computer usage –

specifically the porn sites he frequents. Evidently he has broken the law because some of the sites he has visited have underage girls. Their explanation for their investigation was that he may have committed a sexual act with a child sometime in the past that the authorities do not have knowledge. In short, they wanted to investigate whether or not he is or was a predator of children.

So let's break this down – there is no specific crime that he's being investigated for but instead he's being investigated because of something he MIGHT have done based on the fact that he frequents porn sites?

If I follow that line of thinking then I might be a murderer in an undiscovered crime because I read a lot of murder mysteries? I also keep a gas-guzzling car in my garage, so I might have committed a potential crime against the environment?

I'm not in favor of porn sites. I hate them. They are the ultimate of exploitation of both sexes and all children. Often the participants are not willing or consenting; they are drugged and forced into performing for the camera. I wish I had the power to shut them all down. But my singular disgust and condemnation will not prevent them from staying in business.

I questioned Riley about the porn sites he visited and he told me that he will go to a free site, since I don't put money on his credit card for him, then he will click on one of the sites advertised on the side bar. Most of the time these sites will offer a certain number of "free trial" days before a charge appears on the credit card. Riley has a pre-paid card that has no money on it. He uses the card info to obtain the free trial and then the card is declined when the site tries to charge the subscription to it.

In the toxin soaked mind of a resident of Riley World. This routine is perfectly acceptable. When Riley was told that most of the females on these sites are most often underage girls, Riley vehemently denied that this was child pornography. He states that there is always a little blurb stating that all the people featured on all the sites he views are of legal age. Riley believes disclaimers. He honestly truly believes that these sites would not lie to him.

One of the agents asked Riley about one of the titles of the sites he frequents because it says something about babies. Riley stands by his assentation that the title is just a way to draw people in. He says that it is all just role-playing. He insists that everything is just consenting adults. He has never seen anything about babies on that site or any other site.

I think what most upset me about the interview with the officers, was that I felt they were trying to slip me up in some way or another. They couldn't or wouldn't give me the information I needed to be able to assist them in their investigation. They had no specifics of any crime except the viewing of porn. That was bothersome. But not as bothersome as the reaction of one of the investigators when I tried to explain that Riley's brain did not function as a normal person.

I asked if they had any knowledge about what happens to the brain of a person who is an end-stage alcoholic or even an alcoholic who has consistently abused alcohol over a long period of time. The answer was NO. I was dismayed by that answer because it feels that they are doing a job without information that could affect their investigation.

I proceeded to explain about how the alcoholic toxins lodge in the frontal lobe and create a situation of loss of common sense, loss of moral compass, loss of memory, etc. I explained how it happens and how it incapacitates the alcoholic from following through on most of his thought processes. In effect the alcoholic is brain-damaged. I stressed that whatever he was discussing with Riley today, would most likely not be remembered tomorrow. He has a memory window of about eight hours before simple things must be repeated. I explained that the questions being asked him about different timelines would probably not be answered accurately because Riley sometimes doesn't know what he did when. If they wanted to know where he was and when, they would get more information from me than from Riley in spite of the fact that we were physically separated for those 15 years.

I thought they understood. I thought I had gotten through to them – until the officer with the crinkled up, confused forehead said to Riley that he imagined Riley was a smart guy – he had managed a submarine career, went to college, and has been a member of Mensa... so he knew what was what. He said that surely Riley understood what was going on in the interview. Riley nodded his head in affirmation.

I wanted to stand up and scream – "DO YOU NOT GET IT?" It doesn't matter how smart Riley was in a previous life. He is brain damaged and doesn't have the same capacity he did 20 or 30 years ago. Alcohol destroys that. So he may understand in that moment when the officers were present, but he doesn't truly understand what he is doing is wrong. His brain doesn't allow him to make that connection.

The investigator states that he must ascertain if Riley is a threat. My response was "Did you not drive out here? Take a look around? Do you see any schools? Any children? ANYONE else? He doesn't drive. We are in the middle of nowhere. There is NO one for him to physically harm."

The crowning piece from that same officer, was that "Well, you don't seem so drunk today. You seem like you have it together."

Are you kidding me?????? He's a drunk. He's end-stage. He's NEVER sober. It doesn't matter what he looks like or how much he has drank today – he's not in a reasonably sane state of mind. How can any sane, sober person even imagine that a person who drinks 14-16 cans of beer, a half-gallon of wine, and/or a liter of vodka a day is anywhere near "being OK?" I don't know who is more unreasonable – Riley or the crinkle-foreheaded investigator.

Here's the bottom line – based on what I know about Riley, I sincerely doubt that he has ever done anything that would resemble molestation. The possibility of him molesting anyone now is so remote that it's ridiculous. Do I think he might be sexually attracted to teen girls in the 16-18 age range? Of course I do. Do I think he would prefer to be with them rather than a woman with large breasts who has a decent vocabulary and will pay his way through a date? Absolutely not.

Let me be clear – in my opinion, anyone who commits a crime against a child should be prosecuted to the fullest extent of the law. Children should be protected at all costs and I'm willing to give up some personal freedoms to make that happen. I would not protect Riley if I had any reservations about his sexual conduct. As disgusting as I find his sexual interests to be, I doubt children would ever fit into the equation.

As far as the law enforcement personnel are concerned, I believe that they should be knowledgeable. As with my issues with medical professionals – it seems the law enforcement community is sorely lacking in addiction education as well.

Unfortunately, 99% of the wives that I communicated with from my blog tell me that their end-stage alcoholics watch an excessive amount of porn. I don't think that because they watch the porn that they are absolutely child molesting predators.

I'm not saying that all alcoholics are not predators – I'm very sure that most predators are probably alcoholics. That would be like saying EVERYONE who loves chocolate is fat. I know lots of really skinny people who eat far more chocolate than I do while I'm on the fatter side and have very few cravings for chocolate at all.

After they left and I had time to think about everything, I began to feel that I had no privacy in my home. I wondered if my phone was tapped or if they would access the tracker in my car. For the first time ever, I closed all my blinds, checked that all windows and doors were double locked, cleared my computer history and temporary files, and didn't answer my phone or make any calls. And, just to be sure, I checked the map to confirm that North Carolina was still a part of the United States.

I've been assured that my computer activity is of no interest to the investigation. I even let the investigator's computer guy check to verify that nothing had been accessed from my password protected computer. He said my computer was of no interest to them. But still, if they were investigating only Riley for being a potential predator – why do I feel that I've just been raped??

THERE'S ROOM ON
THE ROLLER COASTER

I was in my office, as usual, when I heard the crashing of items tumbling to the floor. Riley had fallen. Again. It had become an everyday occurrence in our house. Riley falls and I can't pick him up, so he lies there until he can manage to regain an upright stance. It's become part of our daily routine.

I peeked into the den and found Riley with his head resting up against the brick hearth of the fireplace. Oh!! This time it was really bad! After every fall Riley will mumble "I'm OK" and he stayed true to form. But, he didn't look OK. He looked like a bloody mess. He was bleeding from his forehead and arm and he had scrapes down the side of his face.

The next morning he looked even worse than he had the day before. His eye was swollen shut and his face was swollen. I asked if he wanted to go to the emergency room. NO – he did not. I asked if he would go see our primary care doctor. To my surprise, he said he would go. The appointment was made for that afternoon and off we went to town.

Erica examined Riley's bumps and bruises and made the determination that he had not broken any bones. The thing to watch for was excessive sleepiness, slurring of words and confusion. I'm not sure how I would know if those things were happening, because that's how he is every day. They did some blood work and then we left.

When the results of the blood test came back, everything showed to be as Erica expected for an end-stage alcoholic. Copies of the test would be mailed to me.

A couple of months later, Riley fell getting out of the van. He fell hard onto the pavement landing on his right arm against the brick steps. I thought he had broken his arm. It was swollen and bruised and he was in a lot of pain. He consented to another doctor's office visit.

The arm was not broken, but it would take a long time to heal. Once again, they took another batch of blood. This time the results were not mailed to me. Instead I got a phone call from Erica telling me that I MUST get Riley to the hospital immediately. His potassium levels were extremely low and he was in danger of having a heart attack. There was some discussion back and forth and finally Riley said he would go, but he didn't want to detox.

He spent the night in the hospital getting his potassium replenished while I got a wonderful night's sleep. He came home and that was what I thought would be the end of it. Erica had arranged for us to have a visiting nurse to help with the aftermath of the recent falls. I felt that someone had finally listened to me and was willing to provide me with some help.

For the first time in more than 18 months, Riley had a shower. It was assisted by a bath aide who simply managed to get him undressed and into the shower stall. Riley would never take a shower simply because I asked him to. But, he would take a shower if he had an outsider come in and help him with it. I didn't care – he no longer smelled of something rancid.

The nurse noticed Riley's heart was not beating correctly. She used the term erratic and suggested we go back to the doctor to have it checked out. So off we went. Erica used the stethoscope to listen to Riley's heart. She had to keep asking him to stay quiet so she could hear what was going on inside his chest. Satisfied with her findings, she said that there was nothing wrong his heart. That was good enough for us.

We continued to have the nurse and bath aid on a weekly basis. At every visit the nurse would listen to Riley's heart and then shake her head. She didn't understand why Erica had not been able to hear what she was hearing. After several weeks, I asked her if I should get a second opinion. Since she thought it might be a good idea, I made an appointment with my cardiologist.

In the ensuing weeks, an echocardiogram was done and Riley wore a Holter heart monitoring device. The results of the echocardiogram showed that Riley's heart did not have anything major going wrong, but we still didn't have the results of the Holter. I was frustrated and simply didn't know what to do and conveyed the feelings to the physician's assistant. She set up a group meeting for the all of us to come to some kind of agreement as to what could be done for Riley.

I was hoping for him to get detoxed and then sent to a long term care facility. That was not to be. When Riley stated that he refused to quit drinking, even though he would go to detox, the doctor stated that he would have him committed. Unfortunately the commitment would only be for the detox and not long-term care. The chances were that he would be discharged from detox and sent home to repeat the cycle.

The frustration was just way too much for me and I blurted out – "Why can't we just let him die?!?" It was clearly what he wanted. He had said it over and over again – if the choice is death or sobriety, he wants death.

Dr. White asked me what I needed that he could provide. I told him the nurses were due to stop in a week and asked that he extend that time for me. He said YES. Then told me if I needed anything else to let him know and he would provide it. I thought maybe I should ask for a winning lottery ticket, but decided that might be a bit too much to ask. For now, I settled on the nurses.

In the background, while I was trying to talk to Dr. White, Riley is loudly stating that he just wants to be left alone to drink himself to death without interference. He says he wants to get in his car and leave me so he can live his life his way. The voice created chaotic noise and no one was responding to his demands.

Things were quiet on the way home for a few minutes until Riley asked when I was going to make a dentist and optometrist appointment for him. He also stated he needed a haircut, manicure and pedicure and that I needed to make sure those things happened.

I pulled the car off the road and turned off the ignition. I spun around and looked him in the eyes. "There will not be any more doctor appointments of any kind. You have chosen death. You're like an old car that needs a lot of work, but won't last even if the work is done. There is no point in you going to any more doctors. I will not take you." I continued to tell him that since he wanted to be "left alone" I would grant him his wish. I would no longer cook, clean up his messes, do his laundry, or be his servant in any manner. The only thing I would do is buy him his booze because it had become vital to keeping him alive and I truly did not care about his health anymore. We drove the rest of the way home in silence.

It had been a couple of weeks since I stopped cooking for him. He was losing weight quickly. When Janet, our nurse, came to see him she told him he was dying in front of her eyes. With each visit, she asked him if he knew that he was dying.

"I know I'm dying. We are all dying. But, I will still be here for another 30 years when I will be shot by a jealous husband." Riley was firm in his belief that he had not yet reached his expiration date.

There was nothing more she could do for him. She said she would put in a request for hospice care.

I had not cleaned his bathroom in that time and dirty diapers were spread out all over his bathroom floor. There were feces on the walls and on the light switches. The bath aide called, but I told her the bathroom had not been cleaned. She informed Riley that she would not come if the bathroom was not sanitary. There was no longer anything she could do for him.

It seemed there was no longer anyone who could do anything for Riley — doctors, nurses, aides, counselors, me — there was nothing any of us could do that would improve or extend his life. Riley was getting what he wanted — to live out the end of his life in a drunken stupor. He would die a lonely old man, just as had been predicted many years before.

HOORAY FOR HOSPICE...
BUT WAIT...

Janet made a referral to hospice care and Dr. White made the order. Tonya and Tammy visited our house to make the evaluation and prepare for his admittance.

They explained that it was their job to make sure Riley's wishes were carried out. They would not promote his death, but they also would make no attempts at saving it. He had an advance directive and DNR in place. Riley had clearly stated his choices. They told me that the decision as to "what to do" was no longer my decision and I was no longer expected to go against my basic beliefs in order to grant him his wishes. It was now their job and only their job to provide Riley with what he wants.

I was told that every effort would be made for me to not witness the very end – unless – of course – I wanted to be there. I did not. Unfortunately, Riley may not reach the point where his end will be peaceful. Instead I may be forced to be a witness if he has a seizure or bleeds out. If they cannot get here in time, I may have to watch it all go down. I was instructed not to call 911, but to call a specific phone number directly to hospice. I was given bright pink papers to be placed near the phones as a reminder of what to do and who to call.

Tonya and Tammy toured my house so they would know what rooms were where. If I called and said Riley was in the pantry, they would know exactly where he was and the quickest route to reach him. We decided on setting up a hospital bed in the guest room where there would be plenty of room for them to get all the way around it. There would be room for a bedside commode and any other pieces of equipment.

There were papers to be signed, releases, authorizations, statements... Tammy handed me her pen... I hesitated and glanced back at Riley. He was sitting in his rocking chair and had been listening to most of the interview. There was no expression on his face or in his eyes that told me anything. He was blank.

My mind flashed back to signing the papers that allowed my son's life support to be terminated so he could die. I relived the trauma of what was, in my mind, killing my own son. I flashed further back to my older brother begging me to pull the plug that was keeping his non-functional body in a hospital bed with no hope of survival. It all came rushing back to me... all the funerals, tears, faces of loved ones who have already passed. I could feel every hole in my heart that had never mended.

The tears were flowing hard now... my shakey hand grasped the pen and I asked "where?" "Right here, we'll do it together" replied Tammy as she took my left hand in hers. She pointed to the signature line on each paper and I signed each one. I handed her back the pen.

I was surprised at what happened next, I had an overwhelming feeling of relief. This heavy burden was no long on my shoulders. I could take a deep breath. But, I was also feeling guilt. I still felt I was taking another person's life. I told Tammy what was going on inside my head. She told me my feelings were normal. But my reaction was so much more emotional than most other caretakers; she asked me what I had been thinking about.

The story of my family's succession of rapid fire memorial services fell from my mouth out onto the table. Tammy was amazed. There were so many. So much more than most have to face in an entire lifetime. The spacing between the deaths never let me recover from one before being hit in the face with another. She explained that this was a "stacked loss" which could resemble a form of Post-Traumatic Stress Disorder. The agency has a grief counselor who specializes in multiple death scenarios. She asked for my permission to have this counselor meet with me.

Riley was examined, a blood sample was taken and an attempt was made to communicate to him what was about to happen and how it would take place. Riley repeated he was fine with everything except that he wasn't going to die. He wanted to know what would happen when six months had passed and he was still alive. Tammy told him he would be re-evaluated and hospice would continue.

I was still searching for some hope in Riley's face while Riley was being examined. I was still looking for a sign that said "WAIT!! I've changed my mind! I choose life!" But it simply was not there. The sweet smile that he once had was not there. There was no sparkle in his brown eyes. There was no acknowledgement or sense that he truly understood that his life would probably be ending before Christmas.

On Friday morning I received a phone call from Tammie. She said there was good news and bad news. The bad news was that Medicare would not consent to payment for hospice because Riley's Albumin level was a half point too low. He needed to be at point 3 and he was 2.5. The hospice service had been cancelled. I didn't ask what the good news was because I imagined that it was supposed to be good that Riley was "not that bad" yet. For me, the burden was back on my shoulders and it felt heavier than ever.

I thought "But, of course. He is the Immortal Alcoholic."

HAVE A HEART

Saturday seemed to be a difficult day for Riley. He was falling almost every time he tried to stand up. He fell out of his bed. He fell while fixing a drink. Finally, he decided he'd just go to bed and stay there. I fixed him a drink with a straw and arranged things around him so he wouldn't have to get up.

It was about 11:00 pm on Saturday night when I could hear Riley calling to me. I had been able to fall asleep easily that night and felt some resentment for having to get up.

Riley was in his bed, lying on his side, his breathing was labored and I could see the fear in his face. "Please, Linny, call 911... I can't breathe."

I hesitated. I reached for the phone. I thought that if this had been one day sooner, I'd be calling the hospice emergency number. I looked at Riley struggling for each gasp of air. Suddenly, I was at a loss of what to do next. Do I do nothing and watch him die? Maybe he wouldn't die. Maybe it was just a passing thing. He always seems to survive no matter how bad it looks.

Inside my mind, I was still debating as to what I should do. As I dialed in the numbers 9... 1... 1... I was still thinking that maybe I should just ignore his request. At that moment it seemed there were two Linda Jane's in the room. One would let him struggle and die. The other would follow her moral compass and get him help. It was as though I thought I actually had some control over the situation. To a sane person, it would be clear that I had no control nor did I ever have any control. But the insanity of alcoholism always slops over onto the caretaker.

Riley was loaded into the ambulance and I met him in the emergency room of our little tiny glorified band-aid station of a hospital. The doctors and nurses were efficient and tended to Riley promptly. In a matter of minutes, Riley was loaded into a helicopter and taken to the best cardiac hospital within 3 hours of us.

I knew he was in good hands. I knew there was nothing more I could do at the moment. I went home, showered, put some things into a bag and started off on the long drive to the hospital.

There is something about driving down a long road that you've driven many times. The mind starts to wandered. A lot of thinking can be done. Scenarios can be played out. Ideas and creativity can come to the forefront. Options become clear and concise. And decisions can be made.

Riley was in the cardiac intensive care unit of the hospital. His room was very large with a lot of open space around his bed. There was a little alcove with a love seat and recliner. A TV was hanging on the wall visible only by the alcove visitors.

Riley was barely conscious and struggling to hang onto life. Two doctors entered the room. One spoke in a language that I did not understand. It was a medical-eze with terms and explanations that made no sense to me. After the non-understandable doctor left the room, the other spoke to me like I was a real person.

The bottom line was that even if Riley survived the heart attack, his life would never be the same. The liver damage was too extensive and his other organs may start to shut down. If he had a code blue, and they revived him, he may not come back as anything more than a vegetable. In short, he wanted to know if Riley had an Advance Directive and how far did I want the staff to go to save his life.

259

Fortunately, there was a directive in place and Riley agreed to a DNR. As he was signing the form, he stated it didn't make any difference because he still had 30 more years to live. It wasn't his time to go yet.

The next day, Riley was transferred to a lower level of care. He was placed into the ICU. The hospital social worker called and said the family needed to get to the hospital right away. She believed Riley was within hours of death.

We all converged on the hospital, me, Alea, Ryan and Nicole. We visited him and told him it was OK for him to go. We waited and waited.

Riley was moved to the Palliative Care Unit and we waited some more. Ryan patiently fed him water and applesauce. Nicole, Alea and I went to the cafeteria and sat in the garden just outside Riley's room. Eventually, the nurse came to us and told us that Riley was in good hands and since he didn't even seem to know we were there or who we were, maybe we should go home and get some rest. After all, this could be a long process.

I had planned to return to the hospital the next day, but received a phone call that Riley was being transferred to the hospice care home that was under the hospital venue. I needed to make phone calls and push for Riley to be placed under Veterans Administration care. It took two days before I was informed that the VA would, in fact, take over his care and have him transported to an approved facility.

The agency that was to provide hospice care previously was chosen as the one to provide him care under VA supervision. A nursing home was chosen that was within 30 miles of our home. There were papers to be signed, interviews and meetings. There seemed to insurmountable miles of red tape. I plodded on through each hoop and dotting every single "I".

My days are different now. Riley is in the hands of the nursing facility, hospice and VA. There isn't much more I can do for him except visit every other day. I make sure he gets bathed and that he is in clean bed linens. But, mostly I just wait.

Visiting Riley really isn't so bad anymore. He always has some outlandish story to tell me about what he did the night before. Usually he thinks he went to a residential fire but could not get out of the truck. Sometimes he believes we live in Pennsylvania and other times it's Indiana or just "somewhere". He never says we live in North Carolina, but knows we live in the country. He believes the staff is moving his bed around to different rooms during the night. He complains that timbers are being removed from the walls and used elsewhere in the facility. I'm told the brain damage is most likely permanent.

The Riley I met in 1967 that was handsome and debonair, intelligent and conversational, logical and reasonable, and once told me if he couldn't hold me in his arms he would hold me in his dreams – that Riley – he died a long time ago. I would see glimpses of him throughout the years and I would be drawn back into his chaos. I longed so much for each glimpse to become reality that I would fall for him over and over again. Hope is alluring. Hope is intoxicating. Hope is addictive. Hope without the tempering of reality can be heartbreaking.

Riley now sits in a nursing home where his life will probably never get any better than it is today. I'm told he is dying. I'm told he cannot last much longer. No one tells me how long "much longer" really is in the grand scheme of things.

My distrust of the medical community is obvious because I seem to always be asking if they are sure he is dying. Each time I visit, he appears to look physically better. I explain my experience and theories of his liver regenerating and his returning to a healthy life.

But, each time I'm told that it just isn't possible and they patiently explain why it isn't possible. But still… I keep in mind that he is the Immortal Alcoholic.

THE END

POST SCRIPT

OARS F&F SUPPORT GROUP

If you are struggling as the caretaker of an end-stage alcoholic, I urge you to join the OARS F&F Support Group on Facebook. This private group is open only to those who have sent an e-mail to me at immortalalcoholic@gmail.com and explained a bit about their situation. They must then request permission to join with permission granted, usually, within 24 hours.

The people in this group share and support each other in ways that just can't be managed elsewhere. The only rule is to treat each other with respect and consideration. We do not pass judgment and we do not criticize. Please join us!

SEQUEL

There may be a sequel to this book. I haven't decided yet. But in my heart, I don't really think this journey will be complete until I have a death certificate in my hand.

DISCLAIMER

Nothing in this book was intended to be defamatory in nature to any person, place, facility or group. Of course, we all cross people in our lives that may cause us to be uncomfortable and sometimes relationships can create uneasiness. If I have offended anyone in the writing of this book, please accept my heartfelt and sincerest of apologies as that was not the purpose of my words.

RILEY'S REHAB / DETOX JOURNEY

1983   U.S. Navy Alcohol Rehabilitation Center – Norfolk, VA (Detox & Rehab) Actively participated in AA

1987   Veterans Administration Medical Center, Hampton, VA (Detox)

1988   Veterans Administration Medical Center, Hampton, VA (Detox)

Half-Way house, Hampton, VA (Rehab)

1989   Portsmouth Psychiatric Hospital(Detox & Rehab)

1992   Hampton, VA -- Court ordered rehab after second "drunk in public" arrest

2003   The Center for Recovery (Near fatal Detox & Rehab)
Actively participated in AA

2008   The Center for Recovery (Near fatal Detox & Rehab)

2009   Menifee Valley Hospital (Near fatal Detox)

2010   Chesapeake General Hospital (Near fatal Detox after stroke)

2012   Chowan Valley Hospital (Heart issues)

2012   Greenville Heart Hospital (Heart attack)

WEBSITES AND REFERENCES

I have found the following websites to be instrumental in obtaining information.

GENERAL INFORMATION

1. www.nlm.nih.gov

2. http://www.emedicinehealth.com/alcoholism/article_em.htm

3. http://www.ncbi.nlm.nih.gov/books?term=alcoholism

4. www.pubs.niaaa.nih.gov

5. http://en.wikipedia.org/wiki/alcoholism

6. http://www.ehow.com/about_5041054_symptoms-end-stage-alcoholism.html

7. http://www.alcoholism-facts.com/end-stage-alcoholism.php

8. www.recoverymonth.gov

SUPPORT SITES, FORUMS and BLOGS

9. www.immortalalcoholic.blogspot.com

10. https://www.facebook.com/groups/273999545981419/28323
    3241724716/?ref=notif&notif_t=group_activity#!/groups/27
    3999545981419/283233241724716/?notif_t=group_activity

11. http://www.nursepractioner.org/addiction-blogs

12. http://www.hypercryptical.blogspot.com/

13. http://www.alcoholicdaze.blogspot.com/

14. http://fine-anon.blogspot.com/

15. http://texandave.blogspot.com/

16.   http://gerry-daughters-of-the-shadow-men-ii.blogspot.com/

17.   www.sober.com

18.   www.community.aetv.com

19.   http://www.the-alcoholism-guide.org/alcoholism-questions.html

20.   http://www.thriveinlife.ca/thrive

21.   www.al-anon.org

22.   www.aa.org

23.   www.alcoholism.com

24.   www.alcoholism.about.com

25.   www.recoverymonth.gov

MEDICAL INFO

26.   www.webmd.com

27.   www.pubs.niaaa.nih.gov

28.   http://en.wikipedia.org/wiki/alcoholism

29.   http://www.the-alcoholism-guide.org/alcoholism-questions.html

30.   http://www.egetgoing.com/Drug/5_9_2_1_2.asp

31.   http://www.ehow.com/about_5041054_symptoms-end-stage-alcoholism.html

32.   http://www.alcoholism-facts.com/end-stage-alcoholism.php

33.   http://providentliving.org/pfw/multimedia/files/pfw/pdf/12 2750_15BPHLR_pdf.pdf

34.   www.fsis.usda.gov/factsheets/parasites_and...**illness**/index.asp

35.   www.en.wikipedia.org/wiki/**Human_feces**

36.   www.en.wikipedia.org/wiki/**Human_waste**

LEGAL STUFF

37.   http://www.caringinfo.org/i4a/pages/index.cfm?pageid=3289

38.   http://ag.ca.gov/consumers/pdf/AHCDS1.pdf

39.   http://www.medicinenet.com/script/main/art.asp?articlekey=46355

40.   http://www.doyourownwill.com/living-will/states.html

41.   http://estate.findlaw.com/estate-planning/living-wills/le23_9_1.html

42.   http://www.expertlaw.com/library/estate_planning/durable_power_of_attorney.html

43.   http://www.uaelderlaw.org/advance/7.html

44.   http://www.clearleadinc.com/site/power-of-attorney-form.html

ABOUT THE AUTHOR

LINDA BARTEE DOYNE started the Immortal Alcoholic blog as LindaJane Riley, the wife of a seemingly immortal alcoholic, out of respect for her husband's anonymity. Since then he has given her permission to use her real name.

Linda is a blogger and support group founder. She is active in providing information and resources to the often-overlooked group of people involved in alcoholism – the caretakers of the end-stage alcoholics.

A native of Northern California, Linda makes her home in Eastern North Carolina where she can be close to her daughter, grandchildren and great-grandchildren.

Made in the USA
San Bernardino, CA
02 February 2019